GCSE in a week

ISLINGTON LIBRARIES

3 0120 01742740 2

D1646377

History

Series editor: Kevin Byrne,
Abbey Tutorial College

Where to find the information you need

SUCCESS OR YOUR MONEY BACK

Letts' market leading series GCSE in a Week gives you everything you need for exam success. We're so confident that they're the best revision books you can buy that if you don't make the grade we will give you your money back!

HERE'S HOW IT WORKS

Register the Letts GCSE in a Week guide you buy by writing to us within 28 days of purchase with the following information:

- Name
- Address
- Postcode
- Subject of GCSE in a Week book bought
- Probable tier you will enter

Please include your till receipt

To make a **claim**, compare your results to the grades below. If any of your grades qualify for a refund, make a claim by writing to us within 28 days of getting your results, enclosing a copy of your original exam slip. If you do not register, you won't be able to make a claim after you receive your results.

CLAIM IF...

You're a Higher Tier student and get a D grade or below.
You're an Intermediate Tier student and get an E grade or below.
You're a Foundation Tier student and get an F grade or below.
You're a Scottish Standard grade student taking Credit and General level exams, and get a grade 4 or below.
This offer is not open to Scottish Standard Grade students sitting Foundation level exams.

Registration and claim address:
Letts Success or Your Money Back Offer, Letts Educational, Aldine Place, London W12 8AW

TERMS AND CONDITIONS

1. Applies to the Letts GCSE in a Week series only
2. Registration of purchases must be received by Letts Educational within 28 days of the purchase date
3. Registration must be accompanied by a valid till receipt
4. All money back claims must be received by Letts Educational within 28 days of receiving exam results
5. All claims must be accompanied by a letter stating the claim and a copy of the relevant exam results slip
6. Claims will be invalid if they do not match with the original registered subjects
7. Letts Educational reserves the right to seek confirmation of the Tier of entry of the claimant
8. Responsibility cannot be accepted for lost, delayed or damaged applications, or applications received outside of the stated registration / claim timescales
9. Proof of posting will not be accepted as proof of delivery
10. Offer only available to GCSE students studying within the UK
11. SUCCESS OR YOUR MONEY BACK is promoted by Letts Educational, Aldine Place, London W12 8AW
12. Registration indicates a complete acceptance of these rules
13. Illegible entries will be disqualified
14. In all matters, the decision of Letts Educational will be final and no correspondence will be entered into

The Author and Publisher are grateful to the following for permission to reproduce copyright materials: page 5 (text) Penguin UK (both photographs) Mary Evans Picture Library; page 20 Weidenfeld and Nicolson; page 28 Centre for the Study of Cartoons, University of Kent and Solo Syndications Ltd.; page 87 Weimar Archive; page 89 Magnum Photos

Letts Educational
Aldine Place
London W12 8AW
Tel: 020 8740 2266
Fax: 020 8743 8451
e-mail: mail@lettsed.co.uk
website: http://www.letts-education.com

Every effort has been made to trace copyright holders and obtain their permission for the use of copyright material. The authors and publishers will gladly receive information enabling them to rectify any error or omission in subsequent editions.

First published 1998
Reprinted 1998, 1999 (twice)
New edition 2000

Text © Paul Thomas 1998
Design and illustration © Letts Educational Ltd 1998

British Library Cataloguing in Publication Data
A CIP record for this book is available from the British Library.

ISBN 1 84085 3506

Design, artwork and production by Gregor Arthur
at Starfish Design for Print, London
Editorial by Tanya Solomons

Printed in Italy

Letts Educational is the trading name of Letts Educational Ltd, a division of Granada Learning Ltd. Part of the Granada Media Group.

World War One

Test your knowledge

10 minutes

After the killing of the Austrian Archduke **1**...................... ....
at **2**...................... , the diplomatic crisis swiftly snowballed into war. The
Alliance system ensured that Austria would deliver an ultimatum to
3...................... which would bring her patron, Russia, into the war, while
Austria in turn relied upon Germany. Russia was allied to
4...................... who duly entered the war but doubt remained over Great
Britain who eventually joined in because of a Treaty commitment to help
"gallant little **5**...................... ".

Millions rushed to volunteer for their respective armies. In England, Lord
6...................... appeared in a famous poster stating "Your Country Needs
You". Although volunteers feared they would miss a war that would be "over
by Christmas", the early battles were followed by long periods of
7...................... warfare. The machine guns and artillery wiped out advancing
infantry and little progress could be made. Churchill urged the government
to attack the Turks at **8**...................... , but high casualties and
stalemate resulted.

With fewer volunteers and high casualties, **9**...................... was introduced in
most countries and women supplied much missing labour. The sinking of the
passenger liner **10**...................... helped to provoke **11**...................... to join
the Allies in April 1917, and although German successes and revolution drove
12...................... out of the war, with the Treaty of **13**...................... -
.... in March 1918, the arrival of millions of fresh troops from
14...................... helped the Allies to reverse the gains of the German
offensive of spring 1918 and win the war on the Western Front. Industrial
power and population rather than heroism turned the tide.

Answers

1 Franz Ferdinand **2** Sarajevo **3** Serbia **4** France
5 Belgium **6** Kitchener **7** trench **8** Gallipoli
9 conscription **10** Lusitania **11** USA/America
12 Russia/USSR **13** Brest–Litovsk **14** USA/America

 If you got them all right, skip to page 5

World War One

30 minutes

Improve your knowledge

1 Archduke **Franz Ferdinand's** death was the trigger for war. He was the heir to the Habsburg Empire and so the Austrians were furious and sought diplomatic revenge, if possible, military if necessary. Long-term causes centred upon Great Power rivalry and at first diplomats thought the new crisis would be resolved as easily as the many previous flashpoints.

2 **Sarajevo** is the capital of Bosnia, which was then under Austrian rule. The murder was carried out by the Serbian "Black Hand" gang of Slav nationalists to encourage Bosnian and Slav nationalists to reject foreign Austrian rule.

3 The Slavs' protector, Russia, backed up the small but aggressive power, **Serbia**. The Serbs had been very successful during the recent Balkan wars and were confident of Russian support, but their defiance tilted the balance towards the war because the rigid set of secret alliances which divided Europe would bring Germany in to support Austria, and France to support Russia. The result – world war.

4 The Alliance system was dangerous because Austria was a weak and declining power with an over-reliance on the "newer" industrial and military power of a recently united Germany. Furthermore weak and backward imperial Russia, having lost recent conflicts in the Far East, had increasingly sought compensation in the Balkans, in direct competition with Austria. Worse, the Russians were themselves reliant upon the affluent modern power of **France**. Even worse, France bitterly resented her defeat in the Franco–Prussian War of 1870–71 and the loss of territory to the Germans.

5 Britain was uncertain. She had ententes (understandings) and had held naval and military "conversations" with France and Russia. Her excuse was the commitment in the Treaty of London (1839) to guarantee the neutrality of

Belgium. This neutrality was shattered by the Schlieffen Plan; this required the German army to smash through Belgium in order to invade and beat France as quickly as possible before Russia could formally mobilise.

6 All the combatants' plans involved swift mobilisation of huge forces to rush into their enemies' territories to achieve the expected quick victories. Britain only had a small army but possessed a large fleet. **Kitchener** realised war would last at least four years – time to raise and train a huge army, and to use the fleet to blockade and starve out Germany.

7 **Trench** warfare is the popular image of the war and inspired the war poets such as Wilfred Owen and Siegfried Sassoon. Images of mud, cold, boredom and misery alternated with the horrors of being bombarded by high explosive shells or advancing into murderous rifle and machine gun fire across No-Man's-Land.

8 The war was won and lost among the trenches of the Western front but the Allies desperately tried alternatives. If it had been successful, **Gallipoli** would have opened the route to help Russia win her war, but thanks partly to sheer incompetence, the Allies got bogged down there. It was trench warfare plus heat and flies. Other efforts in Persia (Kut) and East Africa were sideshows, interspersed with humiliating allied defeats. Lawrence of Arabia at least provided headlines.

9 Stalemate and high casualties led generals on both sides to the idea of attrition, i.e. wearing the other side out, the winner being the side with the largest available supplies of troops. **Conscription** was the compulsory call-up of the male population to fight this grim form of warfare.

10 The USA was normally anxious to avoid entanglement with Europe's wars. Several hundred Americans drowned when the **Lusitania** was sunk by a German submarine U-Boat, and although for a while the Germans sensibly suspended all-out submarine warfare, it was such an effective way of damaging Britain which was dependent on shipping for supplies that, in 1917, the submarines resumed unrestricted sinkings and an angry USA entered the war.

11 **Americans** enthused about the "War for Democracy" in alliance with the moderate revolutionaries of Russia in 1917 against the militarist and undemocratic German Kaiser. President Wilson declared idealistic war aims which helped encourage populations grown cynical and war-weary.

12 The Allies feared the more extremist Bolsheviks who took over in **Russia** from October 1917, especially as they made it a priority to leave the war which freed up millions of German troops for a last attack on the Western front.

13 The Russians and the Germans made peace at the Treaty of **Brest–Litovsk**. Its harshness gives some impression of German plans for their settlement in the west, had they won the war, but became a dead letter when they were themselves defeated in November 1918.

14 The combatants had tried air-power, tanks, and submarine warfare but in the end the prospect of millions more reinforcements arriving from **America**, while Germany's own forces dwindled, convinced the German commanders to admit defeat. Only then did the home front in Germany also collapse into revolution.

✔ *Now learn how to use your knowledge*

World War One

Use your knowledge

Read the following sources and study the pictures:

a "Desperately men struggled to get through the wire but only got more enmeshed; their equipment caught on the long barbs and made them helpless. They were picked off at leisure by the German riflemen, bodies jerking in their death throes, in the writhing, twanging wire. I could see that our leading waves had got caught by their kilts. They were killed hanging on the wire, riddled with bullets, like crows shot on a dyke." (Private J. S. Reid, 2nd Seaforth Highlanders, *The First Day of the Somme*)

b "What had been the cost of this first hour? It is impossible to say exactly but probably half of the 66 000 British soldiers who had attacked were already casualties – 30 000 infantrymen killed or wounded in just sixty minutes!"
(*The First Day of the Somme*)

c Photograph of T. E. Lawrence in Arab robes.

THE TRIUMPH OF "CULTURE."

d Poster of "Hun" atrocities.

1 What kind of warfare took place on the Western Front between 1914–1918?

Hint 1

2 What was "No-Man's-Land" in World War One?

Hint 2

3 What do documents a) and b) tell us about the nature of war on the Western Front?

Hint 3

4 Explain the importance of "good morale" in war. What effect were the incidents described in *The First Day on the Somme* likely to have on the morale of British fighting troops and civilians at home?

Hint 4

5 Who is the figure in source c) and why was he famous?

Hint 5

6 What is the purpose of source d)? Relate this purpose to the events described in a) and b) and to the career of the figure in source c).

Hint 5

✔ *Hints and answers follow*

World War One

Hints

1 Types of warfare are usually described by the kind of setting in which the fighting takes place, e.g. desert warfare, jungle warfare, or sometimes by the type of weapon, e.g. submarine warfare, or activity, e.g. siege warfare.

2 Documents a) and b) help illustrate this concept. An examiner wants an explanation which goes beyond a simple description to explain the importance of the concept.

3 A good answer will use the skill of empathy, i.e. you need to put yourself in the place of the witness in source a) and of the people he saw, and to think through the **implications** of source b).

4 Think of the qualities required to be a good soldier. Bravery? Enthusiasm? Obedience to orders? Think through the **consequences** of obedience to orders for British soldiers on the first day of the battle of the Somme. Then think of the role of civilians during a war. What is their relationship to those who actually do the fighting?

5 "Thomas soon realised that what he saw on the Western front was hardly likely to bring recruits flocking to the army … so he went instead to the Middle East where … the romanticised dispatches he produced about Lawrence of Arabia not only became brilliant propaganda, but also grew into one of the most enduring myths of the war, turning Lawrence into a national hero." (Philip Knightley, *The First Casualty*)

World War One

1 Trench warfare.

2 The area between the opposing lines of trenches.

3 Explain, using the documents, the implications of troops exposed to machine guns and artillery fire advancing *en masse* across No-Man's-Land.

4 "Morale" is the feeling of enthusiasm and sense of rightness and justification for a cause, often combined with confidence in success. Soldiers may lose confidence in orders that seem likely to result in certain death or wounds and seem unlikely to produce success. Civilians are usually close relatives of the fighters and are likely to lose confidence in generals and politicians who pursue policies likely to cause casualties without achieving success.

5 T. E. Lawrence, known as Lawrence of Arabia, was a flamboyant and successful leader in a minor area of the World War One fighting. His dramatic image and success attracted publicity in preference to the grim news from France.

6 The poster is a piece of negative propaganda, designed to make the Germans appear brutal and barbaric. This will stir up hatred of the Germans among the British, justifying the violence and killing needed in the British war effort.

Likewise, the pictures (and stories) about Lawrence provided dramatic positive propaganda to play up British successes in the war, and to offset the depression and despair likely to arise from events like those at the Somme.

10 minutes

Test your knowledge

At eleven a.m. on 11 November 1918 the guns fell silent. World War One was over. An **1** _World War_ had been agreed. A lasting settlement was to be set up at the Peace Conference at **2** _the house_ from January to June 1919. Much had changed by then. The Germans had agreed on a settlement based upon the American President, **3**........................ .... 's offer of **4**........................ .... for world peace. When the fighting stopped, Germany's army was intact and German soil had not been invaded. The new **5**........................ government of civilians had taken over from the military and expected to negotiate with the Allies as equals. By January, the army had collapsed. As in Russia there had been a **6**........................ , although the Communist **7**........................ revolt had been defeated.

Meanwhile, the Allies' "Big Four": **8**........................ of France, **9**........................ .... of Great Britain, **10**........................ of the USA and Prime Minister **11**........................ of Italy had been affected by the elections held in autumn 1918. The British had been promised "a land fit for heroes" and were told that Germany would pay for the war damage. The French demanded **12**........................ and also expected payment, while the Italians expected some reward for their sacrifices on the winning side.

Worst of all for the Germans, the President of the USA was weakened by illness and political defeat at home. The settlement was dictated to Germany by the vindictive European Allies.

 If you got them all right, skip to page 12

The peace settlement 1918–1920

Improve your knowledge

20 minutes

1 Examiners expect you to get the facts right, i.e. to recall, select and use relevant knowledge. You will also be tested on your understanding of terminology. You can be asked to explain the difference between an **armistice**, a treaty and a peace settlement. An armistice is only a truce or ceasefire in which enemies agree to stop fighting for the time being.

2 In a treaty, two or more countries make a more far-reaching and formal series of agreements after discussions and negotiations, e.g. the Treaty of **Versailles**, the Treaty of Trianon or the Treaty of Sèvres. A peace settlement covers the whole process from 1918 to 1920. Beware: sometimes "Versailles" is used as shorthand to describe the whole peacemaking process.

3 **Woodrow Wilson** was President of the United States from 1912–20. He had fought an election in 1916 on the promise of keeping the USA out of the war. Having entered the war as a conflict "for democracy", he aimed to create a just peace, but was thwarted by a hostile Congress back home and by grave illness.

4 Wilson set out **Fourteen Points** as the basis for the Peace. The main ones to know are:

- the setting up of a League of Nations

- the banning of secret treaties

- plans for general disarmament

- the fixing of a territorial settlement on the basis of the principle of national self-determination, i.e. the right of each country to set up a government of its own choosing.

5 The new civilian German government was set up at the town of **Weimar**. It was blamed for the loss of the war as well as for the harshness of the peace. Virtually every German institution except the trade unions was hostile to it, yet it struggled on till 1933.

6 In effect, the removal of the Kaiser in November 1918 was a **revolution**, but the left wing of the German Socialists wanted a Soviet style workers' republic and mounted a revolt against the Weimar politicians.

7 **Spartacists** were named after the Roman rebel slave, Spartacus, who led the slave rebellion of the last century BC; this Communist revolt was crushed by the right wing ex-soldiers of the Freikorps, a private army hired by the Weimar civilians.

8-11 You need to name each individual accurately and to give a brief account of their role in the Settlement. With **Wilson** weakened in health and political stature, and with **Orlando** very much an also-ran, **Clemenceau** and **Lloyd George** were the major personalities who influenced the peace.

12 By personal inclination and by political necessity, Clemenceau was concerned simply to hurt Germany, partly for **revenge** and partly to so weaken her that a future war should be impossible.

✔ *Now learn how to use your knowledge*

The peace settlement 1918–1920

Use your knowledge

20 minutes

1 Comparing similarities and differences tests your skills of writing and understanding. For example, briefly point out the differences between the four allies at the end of the war and what they might want from the peace.

Hint 1

   a Britain entered the war in 1914, sent an army to France, made a big contribution to the fighting at major battles such as the Somme and Ypres, had an important and powerful navy and featured in the decisive battles at the end of the war.

   b France was invaded by the Germans, fought throughout the war, suffered terrible casualties, and featured in the decisive battle in 1918.

   c Italy was persuaded by hope of reward to join the Allies in 1915, fought many indecisive battles and suffered heavy casualties away from the main Western Front. Was not invaded.

   d The USA entered the war late (1917) and lost few casualties in the (mainly) 1918 battles. Her loans to the Allies and her final contribution in men and potential were decisive.

2 Knowledge is not enough. You need to explain causes and consequences. What facts are important and why?
For example:

Hint 2

   a Explain the terms: War Debts, War Guilt, Diktat (or dictated peace), and Reparations.

   b Explain the importance of the links between these four terms.

Finally, looking back at the original *Test your knowledge* passage, your understanding of terms and details, similarities and differences, and causes and consequences should enable you to answer the longer question: Why did Germany feel such lasting resentment at the harshness of the Treaty of Versailles?

The peace settlement 1918–1920

Hints

1 a) Despite heavy casualties, the British did not suffer the invasion of their homeland. They had incurred huge debts to America and lost out in trade. War weariness from 1916 had made it difficult to keep troops and civilians enthusiastic about the war effort.

b) France had been invaded and devastated, a third of its manpower killed or wounded. The French were angry, frightened and weakened. They owed huge debts and the northern industrial areas needed to be rebuilt.

c) The Italians had suffered, had been promised rewards, but were seen as a second rate ally who had not been vital to victory.

d) The Americans were distant from Europe and reluctant to get involved. They wanted their money back and to stay out of Europe's messy quarrels.

2 If Germany could be blamed (War Guilt), she could be forced to pay for war debts and damage. The Germans were hardly likely to admit guilt. Such a peace settlement would have to be dictated (diktat) by the Allies. The Allies want to pay their debts and therefore need to be paid reparations. They dictate these payments to the Germans and use War Guilt to justify it.

3 The Germans agreed a ceasefire, thinking their position was strong enough to negotiate a fair peace on the basis of Wilson's Fourteen Points which guaranteed national self-determination, open diplomacy, likely universal disarmament, and an effective and inclusive post-war international organisation. After the ceasefire, revolution and political chaos left Germany helpless without an army and vulnerable to a dictated peace, with Wilson unwilling or unable to help. The European Allies, meanwhile, had promised their voters a mixture of reward for the war effort, and punishment and revenge upon the Germans.

The peace settlement 1918–1920

Answers

1 a) Britain's Lloyd George, if anything, moderated Clemenceau's very tough approach, but insisted on Germany handing over her High Sea's Fleet, scrapping her submarines, and went along with the harsh territorial settlement. Reparations were desperately needed to offset war debts and economic hard times. The British were also keen on the system of "mandates" by which Germany's (and Turkey's) old colonies were handed over to the care of the Allies.

b) The French were determined to weaken Germany to prevent any future invasion. The Germany army was reduced to 100 000 men, her navy drastically reduced and military air force abolished. National self-determination was ignored as the Rhineland was de-militarised to protect the French border. Austria and Germany were forbidden to unite, the Sudetan Germans were pushed into the new state of Czechoslovakia, and other Germans stranded in Danzig and the Polish corridor. Alsace and Lorraine came back to France and other industrial areas were taken over to yield reparations. The French used War Guilt to weaken Germany militarily, territorially and economically.

c) Italy got little for her sacrifices and the Italians were justifiably discontented. Such discontent paved the way for Italian Fascism under Mussolini.

d) Wilson's Fourteen Points were largely ignored, as disarmament was applied unfairly only to Germany. German self-determinisation was overridden, providing future German governments with a powerful appeal to grievances in the Saar Valley, the Rhineland, Czechoslovakia and Poland. American governments opted for isolationism, refused to ratify the Treaty and left the League of Nations fatally weakened at the outset by the absence of America, Russia, and Germany from its membership. The USA obstinately insisted on payment of War Debts, thus perpetuating the reparations system till 1931.

2 War damage and suffering caused deep anger among the Allies. They had won and, with Germany's army absent, were in a position to bully her government. Victors traditionally expected reward for their sacrifice and World War One was the first really modern war where the victors actually suffered as much or more than the losers. There was cause to see German militarism and aggression as, to some degree at least, responsible for the start of the war. Logically, War Guilt then justified the harsh measures imposed on Germany, while the weakness of President Wilson, and the collapse of the German army and state created the conditions suitable for a harsh peace. The high level of War Debts added further excuse and urgency.

3 Cause and consequence is clear. The Germans expect fairness and negotiations but receive harshness and dictation. To go further, a good answer will dig into the argument a bit more and point out the Allies' hypocrisy. The Allies had been keen on military display and aggression before the war, too. The Germans had already paid dearly for losing the war through casualties and damage, so it was unfair to make them pay reparations on top of this. Further, it was unfair to force Germany alone to disarm, to exclude her from the League of Nations, and to force native Germans into the foreign states of Poland and Czechoslovakia.

To go up another level, mention the German "stab in the back" myth where the civilian Weimar government were accused of being the "November criminals" who betrayed the German army by surrendering and accepting a harsh peace. Point out that the Nazis made much of this "betrayal" in autumn 1918 for which they blamed Jews, Communists and civilians and claimed that the German army had not been defeated.

Hitler's rise to power

10 minutes

Test your knowledge

Adolf Hitler had been an unsuccessful Austrian civilian. A failed art student who had never earned a living, he became a good soldier in World War One, though never promoted beyond corporal. He joined the **1**...................... .... in autumn 1919 and through his talents as an orator came to lead it. The **2**.................... .... in Munich in 1923 led to his imprisonment during which he wrote his book, **3**.................... ...., which set out his main ideas. His extreme racial theories included intense **4**........ - .... against the Jews and also hatred of **5**...................... . The National Socialist Party, nicknamed the Nazis, demanded a reversal of the Treaty of Versailles, and modelled its organisation and many beliefs on the **6**.................... of the Italian Mussolini.

During the prosperous years of 1925–29, the movement had little appeal in a Germany under the effective and stable government of Chancellor Gustav Stresemann. However, the **7**.................... .... in America led to economic disaster and high unemployment in Germany. The Nazis prospered in elections to the Reichstag and in Hitler's election campaign against the German President von Hindenburg. Thousands voted Nazi or joined the thuggish SA nicknamed the **8**.................... . The public flocked to huge rallies at **9**.................... or marvelled at the propaganda organised by **10**.................... .... A series of backstairs intrigues led by the Catholic politician **11**.................... and the political general **12** .... , following the years in which Chancellor Bruning had ignored parliament and ruled through decree, now led to an invitation for Hitler to form a government with only two other Nazis in the Cabinet. "We have hired him", Hitler's conservative backers claimed. They spoke too soon.

Answers

1 German Workers' Party **2** Beer Hall Putsch **3** *Mein Kampf* **4** anti-semitism **5** Communism **6** Fascism **7** Great Crash **8** Brownshirts/ Stormtroopers **9** Nuremberg **10** Dr Joseph Goebbels **11** Von Papen **12** Von Schleicher

 If you got them all right, skip to page 20

17

Hitler's rise to power

Improve your knowledge

30 minutes

1 The **German Workers' Party** was founded and led by Anton Drexler. One of many right-wing groups often linked to the Freikorps (the private, usually right-wing armies) that sprang up all over Germany after World War One.

2 With the prestigious help of ex-army chief, General Ludendorff, the **Beer Hall Putsch** was the Nazis' attempt at an armed take-over in Munich in Bavaria, modelled on Mussolini's "March on Rome". It was a failure, but Hitler's speeches in court created a propaganda triumph and confirmed his status as leader.

3 Most of Hitler's ideas were formed by 1924 and changed little over the years. Because party members felt they had to have a copy of *Mein Kampf* it was a massive best-seller which secured Hitler's own finances. It was not useful as a warning because Hitler was too unimportant up to 1933, and once in power many critics assumed these were wild ideas that would be abandoned now that Hitler was "respectable".

4 **Anti-semitism** was very common, not only in Austria and Germany, but also in Poland, France and Russia. Hitler's approach was only unusual due to its terrifying literalness and absoluteness of intention. He really meant what he said!

5 Again, Hitler's ideas were very standard for the time and place. Anti-**Communism** conveniently overlapped with his racial ideas, as many Communists and Socialists in Germany were Jewish and those in the Russian Revolution were either Slavs (seen as inferior) or Jews (e.g. Trotsky, Zinoviev, Kamenev).

6 **Fascism** was very popular in Latin countries such as Italy, Spain and Portugal, and was often connected with extreme conservative ideas associated with military, Catholic, or "male chauvinist" values, i.e. courage, discipline, obedience, paternal or male superiority and authority. Hitler admired Mussolini at first.

7 The **Great Crash** and Depression destroyed Germany's modest prosperity and left millions unemployed and angry. Many joined extreme parties of right and left. Both Nazism and Communism offered discipline, a sense of belonging, the opportunity to fight, and a simple explanation for the unemployed's misfortunes.

8 The SA was vital in Hitler's rise. With 600 000 **Brownshirts** in 1933, Hitler was feared by the conservatives who thought this strength on the street would be crucial if civil war against the Communists broke out as seemed likely.

9 Hitler was genuinely popular with at least one-third of German voters. Mass rallies, like the one staged at **Nuremberg**, were carefully orchestrated, rather like modern day rock concerts, to create a sense of drama, emotion and occasion and to maximise the impact of Hitler's extraordinary charisma as a speaker.

10 **Goebbels** employed all available modern technology, e.g. radio, film, aeroplanes, and mass circulation newspapers to increase the impact of positive propaganda glorifying Hitler's vision of Germany and negative propaganda stirring up hatred of Jews, Communists and foreigners. He achieved mass popularity but no democratic majority. However, once in power after 1933, the Party controlled all the media and was able to manipulate the population very effectively.

11 **Von Papen** was a favourite of the President, von Hindenburg, whose permission for the promotion of Hitler was vital in 1933. He helped negotiate co-operation with the Papacy and survived the war but was increasingly unimportant.

12 **Von Schleicher** was important in undermining the last vestiges of democratic rule in Germany which let in first von Papen and then Hitler, who had him murdered in 1934.

✔ *Now learn how to use your knowledge*

Hitler's rise to power

Use your knowledge

20 minutes

Read the extracts below and answer the questions that follow:

a "The handover of power to Hitler on 30 January 1933 was the worst possible outcome to the irrecoverable crisis of Weimar democracy. It did not have to happen. It was at no stage a foregone conclusion." (Ian Kershaw, *Hitler*)

b "The smoothness with which the murders of 30 June were carried out is eloquent proof that no Roehm putsch was imminent. There was no resistance encountered anywhere… many victims unsuspectingly surrendered of their own accord, having faith in their "Führer". The only shots fired were those of the executioners: often enough the SS commandos were also settling private feuds. The number of victims, officially set at 77, is estimated to have been between 150 and 200." (K. D. Bracher, *The German Dictatorship*)

c "The enemy had another hope, that Russia would become our enemy after the conquest of Poland. The enemy did not count on my great power of resolution. Our enemies are little worms. I saw them at Munich." (Hitler's speech to the commanders-in-chief, 22 August 1939)

1 What was "Weimar democracy"? Why was it in irrecoverable crisis?

2 Why was Hitler's entry into power something that "did not have to happen" and was not "a foregone conclusion"?

3 What event is described in extract b)?

4 To what organisation did most of the victims of these executions belong?

5 Who was Roehm and why might there have been a danger of a Roehm purge? Hint **5**

6 In extract c) who is Hitler describing as "the enemy"? Hint **6**

7 Why might Russia and Germany have been likely to become enemies? Hint **7**

8 What "triumph" has Hitler just achieved by his "great power of resolution"? Hint **8**

9 What was it about the enemies at Munich that made them seem like "little worms"? Hint **9**

 ✔ **Hints and answers follow**

Hitler's rise to power

Hints

1 Up to 1918 Germany was very undemocratic, ruled by the Kaiser through a weak parliament by a government dominated by the military. This Reich was associated with success, expansion and empire until the last days of the war. Defeat in the war was blamed on the legend that the army had been "stabbed in the back" by civilians, Jews and Communists. The civilian government after the war was then associated with the "Great Inflation" of 1923, which wiped out people's savings, and with the economic depression after 1929.

2 In the winter of 1932–33 the Nazi party was running out of money. President von Hindenburg had refused to make Hitler Chancellor, and the party was beginning to lose votes at the elections.

3 Stalin admired this event and modelled his "purges" on it.

4 These rivals of the SS had a similar name and nickname to their rivals.

5 Hitler had good reason to fear Roehm's supporters, and did differ from Roehm in his plans and opinions.

6 Think back to World War One.

7 Think of Hitler's theories about race and space.

8 Hitler had just astounded his enemies by doing the unexpected. Who did Nazis normally fear and hate?

9 After Munich, Hitler had no reason to expect his enemies to be stubborn or obstructive.

Hitler's rise to power

Answers

1 In autumn 1918 the German High Command admitted that the war was lost and relied successfully on the dutiful patriotism of Germany's civilians to take over the government and to negotiate the peace. Socialists and democrats, who had always been shunned by the German ruling classes, formed the government named after the Rhine town of Weimar and were thus forced to take the blame for the humiliating Treaty of Versailles and for the subsequent inflation of 1923. Meanwhile, the civil service, army and legal system of Germany made no secret of their hatred of civilian democratic rule and the partnership of Chancellor Bruning and the military minded President von Hindenburg gleefully adopted rule by decree without consulting parliament in the emergency caused by the Great Depression of 1930. Even before Hitler, few important Germans cared to try to save democratic government.

2 The 1932 election results showed the Nazis were losing votes. The worst of the Depression was already over. Conspirators like von Schleicher and von Papen created the conditions which allowed the Nazis in as a result of their own personal ambitions and through the conservatives' fear of Communism.

3 The Night of the Long Knives, when Hitler eliminated the leaders of the SA and various opponents and personal enemies in summer 1934.

4 The SA, nicknamed the Stormtroopers or Brownshirts, was chief among the victims, as Hitler feared they were plotting against him. The army feared their rivalry and ambitions and certainly their leader, Ernst Roehm, differed in philosophy and ambitions for the future from many of the other Nazis including Hitler.

5 Roehm was an old street fighter who believed in some of the "socialist" or revolutionary ideas of National Socialism and disliked the respectable or pro-business aspects of the party in government. There was, however, almost no evidence of the SA's or Roehm's disloyalty and no signs of any planning for a coup. Himmler's SS and the army stood to gain from Roehm's fall and encouraged much of the distrust which fuelled the murders.

6 The Western powers, i.e. Britain and France.

7 In *Mein Kampf*, Hitler was openly hostile to the Soviet Union and was loudly anti-Communist. He also attacked the Communist Russians on racial grounds for their Slavic and Jewish connections.

8 Hitler, via his new foreign minister, von Ribbentrop, had just accomplished the Nazi–Soviet Pact.

9 Hitler had anticipated and probably wanted war as a result of the Munich/Czechoslovakia crisis of 1938. Yet, in this as in previous diplomatic crises, the Allies had pursued a policy of appeasement and given in to Hitler's demands in a seemingly cowardly fashion. They did seem like "little worms" and Hitler thought they would behave similarly when he threatened Poland in 1939.

The League of Nations

10 minutes

Test your knowledge

During the 1920s there were several attempts to obtain agreement towards general disarmament and an outlawing of aggression. Thus, in 1921 the **1**...................... .... agreed ratios for the building of military navies by Britain, America, Japan, Italy and France. In 1925 the so-called **2**...................... .... between German, France and Belgium, guaranteed by Great Britain, ushered in an era of European co-operation while payment of reparations by Germany were rescheduled by the **3**...................... .... in 1925, and by the **4**...................... .... in 1929. An ambitious plan to outlaw war, called the **5**...................... – .... , was signed by many countries in 1928.

After World War One, the destruction of the old Great Powers led the Allies to try to replace the balance of power with **6**...................... .... by which all countries would join together to defeat potential aggressors. Woodrow Wilson's brainchild, the League of Nations would be the main vehicle for action and would also seek to improve labour relations through the ILO and medicine through the World Health Organisation.

Despite some minor early successes, the League suffered from the exclusion or absence of major powers such as **7**...................... , **8**...................... and **9**...................... , from the start, and from the requirement of unanimity in votes in its council.

Italy flouted the League in 1922 over Corfu and again in 1935 over **10**...................... while Japan invaded **11**...................... in 1931 and walked out of the League without suffering. Hitler took Germany out in 1933 without any comeback, while Italy's aggression in 1935–6 was punished only by ineffective sanctions which just served to reinforce the image of the League's helplessness.

Answers

1 Washington Naval Agreements **2** Locarno Pacts **3** Dawes Plan **4** Young Plan **5** Kellogg–Briand Pact **6** collective security **7** USA **8** Russia/USSR **9** Germany **10** Abyssinia **11** Manchuria

✔ *If you got them all right, skip to page 28*

 **Improve** *your knowledge*

20 minutes

1 Woodrow Wilson's Fourteen Points had envisaged universal disarmament and the Germans were understandably annoyed that they alone seemed to suffer forced disarmament. In 1921–22, at least, the **Washington Naval Agreements** led to some limits to the size of navies. Britain now had to concede equality to the USA in size of fleet, while Japan, France and Italy were recognised as second equal naval powers.

2 The years 1925 to 1929 are sometimes known as the Locarno era in which the German Foreign Minister and Chancellor, Gustav Stresemann worked effectively and amicably with his British and French counterparts, Austen Chamberlain and Aristide Briand, towards the **Locarno Pacts**. The actual agreements stated that Britain, France and Germany recognised each other's frontiers, while Germany also opened discussions with Poland and Czechoslovakia regarding their mutual frontiers.

3 Germany had defaulted on payment of reparations in 1922. France and Belgium had invaded the Ruhr to punish the Germans and to extort payment, triggering the inflation which shattered German post-war economy. The **Dawes Plan** rescheduled but did not reduce reparations payments and it ushered in a period in which German prosperity seemed to be re-established by large sums of American short-term loans.

4 After the Wall Street Crash, the world economic crisis in general and the withdrawal of short-term loans from Europe in particular, plunged the German economy into depression. The **Young Plan** (1929) again reduced and rescheduled reparations but the long timetable with final payments stretching into the 1980s was unrealistic. By 1930, the Hoover moratorium gave the Germans a year off any payment, and shortly thereafter the full onslaught of slump ended any possibility of further payment.

5 The **Kellogg–Briand Pact** marked the highpoint of international co-operation soon to be rendered irrelevant by the slump, the rise of Nazism in Germany, and by Japanese aggression in the Far East.

6 The peacemakers assumed that the collective opinion of all members of the League of Nations expressed in condemnation of aggression, perhaps backed up by punitive sanctions, would be sufficient to deter aggressors. Pacts such as Locarno and Kellogg–Briand were supposed to reinforce such expressions of international opinion and guarantee **collective security**.

7 The Democrat President, Woodrow Wilson, faced an isolationist Congress in which his opponents, the Republican party, had won the 1918 mid-term election. He foolishly presented the Treaty of Versailles to the Senate on an "all or nothing" basis. The Senate refused to ratify it and instead of joining and guaranteeing the future of the League, the **USA** stayed out while maintaining an uncompromising attitude towards Allied War Debts.

8 **Russia** was in the throes of revolution and civil war during the Versailles peacemaking. The Allies intervened to try to overthrow the Bolshevik government and left the Soviets in diplomatic isolation which only ended with Stalin's Popular Front policy in the 1930s.

9 **Germany,** as the defeated enemy subjected to the diktat of Versailles, was not invited to join the League and was understandably hostile in the circumstances. The more constructive atmosphere of the Locarno era saw her join the League during Gustav Stresemann's Chancellorship.

10 **Abyssinia**, the last remaining independent native state in Africa was subject to an Italian "mandate". An earlier Italian invasion had been humiliatingly defeated in 1896. In 1935, anxious to extend his existing African settlement policy (Italy held Libya and parts of Somalia), and to distract public opinion from economic troubles, Mussolini ordered its conquest, invoking memories of the Roman empire and calling his countrymen to avenge the earlier defeat.

11 Japan had long held military positions and made considerable investments in **Manchuria**. The invasion of 1931 was linked to a simultaneous coup in Tokyo which brought the civilian democracy under military control. Henceforth, Japan was effectively ruled by a form of military fascism and was committed to a course of international aggression. The League sent Lord Lytton to report on the invasion. Aggression was condemned, and sanctions considered but not implemented. The weakened Chinese government was helpless and sooner or later the Japanese were likely to seek further gains on mainland China itself.

✔ *Now learn how to use your knowledge*

Use your knowledge

20 minutes

Read the passage below, and examine the cartoon. Answer the questions that follow:

"I will begin by reaffirming the support of the League by the government that I represent and the interest of the British people in collective security... the League stands, and my country stands with it, for the collective maintenance of the Covenant, especially to all acts of unprovoked aggression."
A speech by Sir Samuel Hoare, British Foreign Secretary, to the League of Nations, Geneva, 11 September 1935.

1 What was the Hoare–Laval Pact?

2 Hoare claims that his government and the British people support the League. How far does the fate of the Hoare–Laval Pact confirm and how far does it refute this statement?

3 The British and French governments were pursuing a foreign policy commonly referred to as "appeasement". Define "appeasement" and present the main arguments for and against the policy.

4 In what ways were the ambitions and attitudes of the Italians and the Japanese similar in the 1930s?

5 Why were Britain, France, the USA and the USSR all concerned about the aggressive policies of Japan in the Far East in the 1930s? **Hint 5**

✔ *Hints and answers follow*

Hints

1 Hoare was the British Foreign Secretary; Pierre Laval was his French counterpart. Both were anxious to keep Italy friendly.

2 The Pact was dropped because British and French public opinion disapproved of the apparent betrayal of the Abyssinians to the demands of Mussolini which made it seem that Hoare was rewarding Italian aggression.

3 Appeasement was a "neutral" word until the 1930s and was a common enough form of policy. Its use in the 1930s made it seem a weak or evil policy. With the evidence of hindsight available it is easy to be critical of the policy, so look at the options as they seemed to be at the time.

4 Remember, both the Italians and the Japanese were on the winning side in World War One. Both were comparatively "new" as modern nations. Also, think Romans and samurai!

5 Think: geography, trade, empire, strengths and weaknesses.

Answers

1 Britain and France had been able to negotiate an understanding with Italy against Germany, known as the Stresa Front (1935), by playing upon German and Italian differences over the future of the alpine Tyrol area which was disputed by local populations of German and Italian speakers. Naturally Mussolini expected the Allies to be sympathetic about his Abyssinian ambitions. Effectively, the British and French were willing to concede most of Abyssinia to Mussolini provided he conceded the fig-leaf principle of a relic of independence to the remainder. Details of the sacrifice of most of Abyssinia leaked to the press and caused an outcry. The Pact was dropped.

2 Clearly a section of the British public was in favour of standing up to aggression and was opposed to the appeasement of dictators. Hoare's willingness to agree the pact with Laval would suggest that he and his government were less reliable supporters of the League and of collective security.

3 Appeasement was the conduct of foreign policy by conceding a potential enemy's demands in order to avoid the risk of war. It was rooted in the commonsense policy of sacrificing the welfare of weak nations to the interests of stronger nations. In Neville Chamberlain's words, "faraway countries of which we know little" might be sacrificed to avoid war.

Arguments against:

1 It was immoral to sacrifice the weak to the strong.
2 It did not work – the aggressor would be encouraged to come back for more and would grow stronger with each concession.
3 It was not necessary – Germany, Japan and Italy would all have been deterred by a tougher stance.

Arguments for:

1 Morality is a luxury when dealing with a superior aggressor.
2 At the time Germany, Italy and Japan all seemed much stronger than they actually were.

3   Britain and France were too weak to defend interests in Europe, the Mediterranean and the Far East – something had to be given up.

4   There was no public enthusiasm for another war after the horrors of World War One.

5   It bought time for rearmament.

6   There were moral arguments for concessions to the Japanese (defending legitimate interests in China); Italy (mandates and interests in East Africa were the moral equivalent of British and French African empires); and Germany (Hitler was usually arguing on the grounds of national self-determination).

4   Both Japan and Italy were offended by their lack of reward at the Treaty of Versailles. Both (like Germany, united in 1871) entered the modern world as nations rather late. Italy became united with Rome as its capital city in 1870, Japan opened up to the modern world under the Mejii dynasty after 1867. Both had had a military and imperial past. Italy had memories of imperial Rome, while Japan remembered the era of warrior knights (the samurai) and their noble military code (bushido). Both had unhappy experiences with democracy. Both had ambitions for empire – Italy through its links to Africa, and Japan with its interests in Korea and Manchuria. Both were affected by economic depression and sought to resolve such problems by aggression overseas.

5   Both Britain and France had empires and investments in the Far East which might be threatened by Japanese expansion. Since the 1890s the USA had been anxious to follow an "open door", policy in the Far East to allow equal access to trade for all major powers, particularly in China. Meanwhile, Japanese leaders were eager to expand and secure Japan's economic interests either by peaceful or military means and either in the direction of a vulnerable China or an unstable Russian empire. The invasion of Manchuria ensured that Japan's solution would be a military one. Russian military successes against Japan in 1936 ensured that future aggression would be at the expense of China.

Russia in revolution

Test your knowledge

10 minutes

At first, the outbreak of World War One seemed to resolve the problems faced by the Russian monarchy. The struggle with Germany was popular. However, Tsar Nicholas II chose an active role as Commander-in-Chief of the army. He was an incompetent chief and when defeat quickly struck Russia's ill-armed, poorly led army, it was the Tsar who was blamed. Worse, he was away at the Front while his German-born wife, Alexandra, attracted criticism for her patronage of the strange monk **1**..................... .

Food riots in February 1917 in **2**............................. .... swiftly led to revolution and the Tsar abdicated. He and his family were kept captive until they were murdered by the Bolsheviks in 1918.

A **3**.................. government was set up, and under the leadership of the Socialist Revolutionary **4**................. .... tried to carry on the war. This was both unpopular and futile. Further defeat in the spring was followed by attempted *coups d'état* by the Bolsheviks (in July) and then by the conservative General **5**.......... .... (in September).

A power struggle had built up between the government and Duma on one hand and the **6**.................. Soviet on the other. Since April, the Bolshevik leader had repeated the slogans of "**7**................., **8**.................... and **9**.................. " and "All power to **10**.................. ".

In the October Revolution of 1917 the Bolsheviks seized power in the capital but when they dismissed the long-awaited **11**..................... .... in January 1918 it was clear there would be a Civil War. Thanks to the surprising military genius of **12**.................. and the **13**............................. .... , and to the cold-blooded use of terror and **14**.............................. , the Bolshevik Revolution finally triumphed in 1921.

✔ *If you got them all right, skip to page 37*

Russia in revolution

Improve your knowledge

20 minutes

1 **Rasputin** was an immoral, drunken and lecherous creature whose intimacy with a Royal Family which included four young princesses and with the unpopular Tsarina herself deeply discredited the monarchy. His hold on them derived from a hypnotic personality and his ability to alleviate the young Prince Alexei's illnesses. By the time he was laboriously murdered by a group of nobles in December 1917 the damage was done.

2 **St Petersburg** had been vulnerable to mass protests during the 1905 Revolution. Protesting crowds were rightly afraid of the Tsar's willingness to use brutal Cossack troops to suppress trouble. However, in 1917 key parts of the local garrison supported the protesters, and even the Cossacks proved unreliable.

3 By definition, a **provisional** government was only temporary and tended to put off important decisions till after the elections which had been promised for the autumn. Until then matters remained unresolved while the different groups of revolutionaries and moderates competed for power.

4 **Kerensky** saw himself as the saviour of the revolution and relied upon patriotism to unite support behind his government. He missed the opportunity to crush the Bolsheviks after their failed coup in July. The freedoms granted by his Provisional Government played into the hands of his many enemies.

5 The revolutionaries were very aware of the history of the French Revolution and many half-expected the rise of a Napoleon-style figure. Monarchists and conservatives openly wanted either a general or the Germans to come and crush the revolution. **Kornilov** made a half-baked attempt to oblige them.

6 From February 1917, the **Petrograd** Soviet became, effectively, an alternative government. Probably more democratic than the provisional government which was formed from the remnants of a Duma elected before the revolution, Kerensky was a member but allowed it increasingly to come under Bolshevik control. By October, they, with their Left Socialist Revolutionary allies, had gained control of the Soviet.

7 Lenin had picked the three simplest and strongest desires of most of the public – **peace**, **land** and **bread**. The masses were sick of war and many of the largely peasant army were anxious to return home and receive their share if there was to be a general distribution of the land.

8 Hunger had driven the revolution out into the countryside but the Provisional government was not trusted to allow the peasants to keep the land.

9 The revolution had been sparked by food riots. Simply, the masses would follow the party that promised to feed them.

10 **Soviets** were, simply, spontaneous councils which sprang up in Russia during the revolution. They had first appeared in 1905 and could be big or small, representing anything from a platoon of troops, to a village, to a province, to a capital city. Lenin was shrewd enough to spot that control of the thousands of Soviets across Russia would give control of the revolution.

11 Following the example of the French Revolution, the Russians decided to hold democratic elections for an assembly which would be summoned solely to create a lasting constitution. By the time the elections were fought, giving clear victory to the Menshevik and Socialist revolutionary parties, the Bolsheviks were in power and moved swiftly to shut the **Constituent Assembly** down, consigning its members, in Trotsky's words, "to the dustbin of history".

12 **Trotsky** was a skilled and popular public speaker who, as a Menshevik, had been a star of the 1905 revolution. He was an effective leader of the Bolshevik army in the Civil War, and was Lenin's chosen successor. Though capable of ruthless violence, he lacked Stalin's talent for political in-fighting and lost out in the later struggle for power.

The original Red Guards had been the Bolsheviks' street-fighters during the early revolution. Mainly made up of industrial workers and at first backed by the notoriously revolutionary sailors from the Kronstadt naval base, they were expanded into an army of millions, the so-called **Red Army**. Former professional Tsarist officers and NCOs were recruited and the Soviet-style informality and abolition of ranks replaced by strict discipline.

 The **Bolsheviks** won because they were united, unlike the Whites (counter-revolutionaries) who represented a wide range of monarchists, moderates, anarchists and foreign powers. Brutal terror and secret police methods were used to punish and intimidate opponents and fainthearts, while, when shortages and hoarding threatened the war effort, "**War Communism**" simply decreed the requisition by force of all necessary supplies and facilities from peasants and the bourgeoisie.

✔ *Now learn how to use your knowledge*

Russia in revolution

20 minutes

Use your knowledge

1. Who were the Socialist Revolutionaries?

   Hint 1

2. What were the main differences between the Mensheviks and Bolsheviks?

   Hint 2

3. Why were the Bolsheviks willing to risk a *coup d'état* in October 1917 and civil war thereafter?

   Hint 3

4. Account for the Allies' attempt to crush the Bolshevik Revolution.

   Hint 4

5. Why did Stalin rather than Trotsky succeed Lenin?

   Hint 5

✓ **Hints and answers follow**

Russia in revolution

Hints

1 You should be able to give a basic definition of "Socialism".

2 They had both been part of the same party. You need to know a little bit about "Communism" to understand the basics of the Russian Revolution.

3 The Bolsheviks were unrepresentative of the mass of Russian opinion and were well aware of the popularity of other parties and of the fears and hatreds of millions of Russian workers and peasants.

4 Bolshevism, at least until 1928, was openly international in approach. Remember, too, that there was a war on, and the Allies needed to concentrate their attention on that.

5 What were the main characteristics of Bolshevism? What did Trotsky stand for? What were Stalin's strengths?

Russia in revolution

Answers

1 Socialism was a nineteenth-century political belief which advocated redistribution of wealth from the richer upper and middle classes to the poorer working classes. It required the working classes to acquire political power through democracy. Democracy could be established by peaceful or violent means, depending upon the extremes to which a particular socialist party was willing to go. The Russian Socialist Revolutionaries based their ideas on the democracy and equality of the Russian peasant *mir* or village council and were therefore very popular among the huge peasant vote.

2 Bolshevik (which means majority) and Menshevik (minority) had been part of the same Russian Social Democratic party. Unlike the Socialist Revolutionaries, they were followers of Karl Marx. His theory of Communism was designed to deal with industrial society in which industrial workers (the proletariat) would overthrow the exploiting class (the capitalists) in a revolution and then redistribute wealth. The split had come when Lenin had insisted that his opinions or orders should constitute the official party line. At the time (1903) the split weakened Russian Communism. In the long term, Lenin's insistence on total party discipline proved the key to success in the revolution and the civil war.

3 It was a question of timing. It was likely that Kerensky's government would soon find the nerve to crush the Bolsheviks and meanwhile elections to the Constituent Assembly (which the Bolsheviks were bound to lose) were looming. In October 1917 they had nothing to lose.

There was armed resistance to the Bolsheviks as early as December 1917, but a major conflict was inevitable when the Constituent Assembly was dismissed in January 1918. The Bolsheviks could not let the Assembly proceed with its many plans and programmes which would have led to their own disappearance or irrelevance, but to reject the Assembly was to defy the popular vote of the bulk of the Russian people who would therefore have to be confronted directly by force.

4   Both Lenin and Trotsky believed firmly in world revolution and in 1918 were relying on revolution spreading to other countries. It was hoped that the revolutions in more advanced countries such as Germany, Austria and Hungary would succeed, and they would then come to the aid of under-developed Russia. Understandably, the Allies were anxious to prevent revolution spreading and opted, in Winston Churchill's words, "to strangle Bolshevism at birth". Further, the West were furious at the Bolshevik withdrawal from the war in March 1918.

5   The demands of the Civil War brought out the most ruthless and undemocratic aspects of Bolshevism. Lenin had never allowed debate or compromise. Now, in wartime he endorsed revolutionary violence, the removal of political and legal freedom and the use of secret police, torture and terror. Both Trotsky and Stalin were happy with such methods. However, Trotsky's reliance on world revolution proved mistaken after 1921 when the revolution in Western Europe collapsed. Further, while Trotsky had been away leading the fighting, Stalin had built up support and his own expertise within the crucial committees and Party institutions which held the real power in Russia as a result of the revolution. The committee bureaucrat outsmarted the soldier.

10 minutes

The Wall Street Crash of October 1929 ushered in the long slump usually called the **1**........................ .... which affected the majority of world economies through most of the 1930s. The stock-market collapsed on Black Thursday and millions of large and small investors were ruined. Prices collapsed too (this is called **2**...................) and unemployment rose in many countries. International trade broke down as countries imposed **3**..................... .... to protect their own trade, at the expense of others. Many governments seemed helpless and because of the theory of **4**................... - .... they were reluctant to interfere with the economy. Many, like the Labour Government in Britain, sought to reduce government spending and actually cut state benefits. The British Liberal party and the Labour extremist Oswald Mosley criticised this and put forward the ideas of economist **5**...... .... who recommended the borrowing of large sums of money to spend one's way out of the slump. Hitler's Nazi government in Germany did something similar by building motorways and great public buildings, and forcing loans from the German banks.

President Franklin D. Roosevelt, newly elected in 1933, took drastic action in the **6**................... .... during which he passed fifteen major laws. His "New Deal" relieved the worst poverty, created work schemes and stimulated economic activity, and reformed financial institutions to try to prevent a repetition of the disaster. Even so, it was the coming of war and consequent **7**................... that brought back full employment in the USA.

 If you got them all right, skip to page 44

20 minutes

Improve your knowledge

1 Since the Industrial Revolution, most modern economies have grown by about two per cent per year. In America in the 1920s the stock market boom had seen excessive growth as investors chased unrealistic and unsustainable profits. When confidence in such hopes of profits collapsed, investors withdrew their money, stock prices collapsed and remaining investors were ruined. Panic-stricken customers tried to secure their money by withdrawing it from the banks which had to close as they literally ran out of cash. Growth went into reverse resulting in the **Great Depression**, nowadays more commonly called "recession".

2 When growth reverses, there is too little money chasing too many goods which nobody wants, or can afford, to buy. Prices go down to chase buyers, profits become small or non-existent, and the result is **deflation**.

3 Tariffs or customs duties have two purposes. One is to raise revenue by taxing import or export of goods. The other, as in the 1930s, can be to protect a country's own trade by artificially raising the price of other countries' goods. Naturally, when many countries tried to price their rivals out of the market by introducing **tariff barriers** to foreign goods, it simply reduced the volume of world trade prolonging and intensifying the Depression.

4 *Laissez-faire* in effect means leaving the economy to run itself without government interference. Enthusiasm for the "free market" was absolute in the 1920s as the stock market rose and easy profits seemed to be made. Roosevelt's predecessor had been reluctant to challenge this theory.

5 **John Maynard Keynes**, an English economist, had long been critical of "classical" economics, i.e. the *laissez-faire* ideas which dominated economics from the eighteenth century onwards. He had challenged the economic arrangements of the Peace settlement with the dangerous relationships between War Debts and Reparations. His basic theory favoured the use of tax cuts, government borrowing and spending and the use of "make-work" schemes to generate economic activity which would lift an economy out of a slump. Because these views challenged traditional economics and because of some similarities with the anti-capitalist ideas of Karl Marx, Keynes' ideas were often rejected as being "communist" in approach.

6 Traditionally, US Presidents had been limited in their willingness to be active in running the economy or passing legislation. There are many checks and balances in the US constitution to limit the power of the President. Roosevelt's first **Hundred Days** in office were famously active and successful because public opinion in America was united in anger at "big business" for helping to create the emergency. Opinion was anxious to take emergency steps to resolve the crisis and the US Congress was willing to help the President take action through legislation and temporarily to override the bias in the US system which usually works against an active presidency.

7 Despite Roosevelt's status as a very popular president, Americans were strongly attached to *laissez-faire* and suspicious of active government. This went for most governments in the capitalist world. However, the threat of war has always been seen as a sufficiently urgent emergency to allow governments to spend money and interfere in the economy to provide necessary armaments. Therefore, not only in the USA but very notably in Germany and the UK, **rearmament** before World War Two helped to create employment and artificially stimulated the economies to recover from the Depression.

✔ *Now learn how to use your knowledge*

20 minutes

Use your knowledge

The New Deal

1 What did Roosevelt do to reorganise the banking and financial system? **Hint 1**

2 How did he help the farmers? **Hint 2**

3 What was done to tackle unemployment? **Hint 3**

4 What was/is "welfare" and what measures did Roosevelt bring in to provide welfare for Americans? **Hint 4**

5 What measures were introduced to improve workers' rights? **Hint 4**

6 What was the "TVA" and what was its significance? **Hint 5**

The Great Depression

7 How important was the Great Depression in contributing to the rise of Fascism and Communism? **Hint 6**

8 To what extent can the Great Depression be seen as a major cause of World War Two? **Hint 7**

✔ **Hints and answers follow**

The Wall Street Crash and the New Deal

The New Deal

1 The chief problems were threefold:
1   The tendency to trade on credit.
2   A loss of confidence among investors that banks could be trusted to repay savings on demand.
3   The sheer shortfall of investment after the Crash.

2 Farmers had over-extended and over-borrowed during the good years of the war and the early 1920s. Furthermore, they were now unable to profit as crop and livestock prices plummeted in the deflation.

3 Given the lack of confidence or investment, no-one was creating jobs in the early 1930s, so it was vital for the government to provide a lead.

4 Think of the problems and emergencies that afflict all people at times in their working lives.

5 Roosevelt was known for his so-called "alphabet agencies". What did they do? How did they work?

The Great Depression

6 Although Roosevelt's "New Deal" was an example of vigorous and largely successful action, other democratic governments around the world seemed much more inept and ineffective in dealing with the economic crisis. Angry unemployed and impoverished voters were liable to look for parties who offered explanations and solutions for the crisis.

7 The answer follows on from the logic of question 1. Remember the context. What were the main causes of World War Two? Where does the Great Depression fit in?

The Wall Street Crash and the New Deal

Answers

The New Deal

1 Some problems solved themselves. For example, many of the smaller banks had been forced to close by 1933. However, the government had to take over the remaining banks temporarily to guarantee depositors that their savings would be covered by the government in future. Roosevelt then reformed the stock exchange and forced credit investors to put up at least 50 per cent of investments in future.

2 Again, many small farms had been repossessed by 1933, usually by the banks themselves. To maintain prices, Roosevelt ordered the destruction of excess stocks of fruit, crops and livestock. Six million pigs were slaughtered to keep up food prices. The Farmers' Relief Act compensated the farmers for this reduction of output.

3 The National Industrial Recovery Act of 1933 set up a series of "make-work" schemes, notably the Public Works Administration which created major public building projects such as roads and dams, while the Civilian Conservation Corps provided hundreds of thousands of temporary jobs. By 1938, however, Roosevelt's government cut such schemes and unemployment rose again, only levelling off with the beginning of war and rearmament. Employers were encouraged to be more positive in their recruitment, while reductions in working hours helped expand employment opportunities.

4 "Welfare" in the USA corresponds to the British social security system. The US provision was late and grudging by British standards but in 1935 a Social Security Act provided Old Age Pensions and Unemployment Benefit. Child labour was abolished, a minimum wage introduced, but there was no provision for sickness or injury.

5   Restrictions on child labour, reductions in working hours and basic trade union rights were a major advance on the combination of *laissez-faire* and intimidation that had characterised American bosses in the 1920s. A minimum wage was designed to limit the worst exploitation, although the details from John Steinbeck's *The Grapes of Wrath* strongly suggest that US employers were easily able to exploit loopholes in the law.

6   The "TVA" was the Tennessee Valley Authority, a vast government-sponsored project involving hydro-electric dams, irrigation and other works designed to revitalise key areas of the South. Other agencies included the CCC (see 3 above), the FERA which ran soup kitchens and the WPA which ran PWA schemes on a smaller scale. They were designed to provide initiative, finance and leadership where the private sector had failed to provide any kind of lead or investment.

The Great Depression

7   The Crash and the slump thereafter arose quite largely from the post-war economic settlement. The war had created over-production of both agricultural and industrial goods, particularly in the USA, while the related arrangements for payment of War Debts and reparations seriously undermined economic stability. The brief prosperity enjoyed by Europe and especially Germany and Austria during the Stresemann era had wiped out the advances made by the Communists and Nazis in the early 1920s. With the withdrawal of US loans, these economies collapsed and both extreme parties grew alarmingly in size, popularity and levels of activity.

The Communist explanation was simple – capitalism was in crisis and must be replaced. The Nazis, similarly, blamed the crisis on Jews, Communists and rogue capitalists, and promised brutal action. Both parties offered uniforms, a sense of purpose and an opportunity for violence. In contrast, democratic politicians were regarded as indecisive. They were considered to have tried and failed. Extreme solutions seemed more attractive.

8 Certainly Depression created the social and economic background which enabled Fascists in Germany and Japan to take power. Rearmament and associated aggressive foreign policy gave German, Japanese and Italian governments an opportunity to tackle unemployment and to stimulate their economies, and provided popular distractions and dramatic successes to offset the problems of Depression. Further, the problems posed by lack of economic growth badly handicapped the Western powers who felt they lacked the resources to match the apparent scale of rearmament achieved by the Fascist powers. Economic weakness was certainly a frequent justification when the Western powers opted for conciliatory "appeasement" policies towards aggression.

The coming of World War Two

10 minutes

Test your knowledge

In September 1938, Neville Chamberlain, the British Prime Minister, returned from **1**.................. , declaring that he had secured "Peace for our time", having agreed with Hitler that **2**.................. should lose the **3**.................. area containing many of her fortifications and 70 per cent of her industrial strength. War had been temporarily avoided and Chamberlain's policy of appeasement seemed vindicated.

Stalin, the Soviet dictator, was disgusted at this surrender and moved to abandon his **4**.................. .... policy and seek agreement with Germany. In March 1939 the Germans marched into **5**.................. causing even Chamberlain to react angrily. Then Hitler moved to demand the Poles give up **6**.................. and the **7**.................. .... As before he emphasised the principle of national self-determination, but Britain and France moved to guarantee Poland.

Hitler was probably over-confident of Allied weaknesses, especially as he outmanoeuvred their diplomats and concluded a surprise pact with the Soviets. To his surprise, the Allies stood firm and on 3 September Britain declared war. Meanwhile, in the Far East, Japan lurked menacingly. By December **8**.................. virtually the whole world would be at war.

Answers

1 Munich **2** Czechoslovakia **3** Sudetenland **4** Popular Front **5** Prague **6** Danzig **7** Polish Corridor **8** 1941

 If you got them all right, skip to page 52

The coming of World War Two

 **Improve** *your knowledge*

20 *minutes*

1 Britain had shown sympathy for Germany's predicament from soon after World War One. Even Gustav Stresemann's government had emphasised the importance of German self-determination and Hitler was usually careful to play upon the perceived injustice Versailles had inflicted upon German-speaking populations cut off by the Treaty from the Fatherland. Chamberlain, perhaps motivated by vanity, had flown dramatically to **Munich** and to Berchtesgarten to negotiate on Czechoslovakia's future. He was partly convinced by 'Mr' Hitler's charm and reasonableness, but also, when occasion demanded, by Hitler's wild and intimidating rages. The Prime Minister received a standing ovation in Parliament on his return from Munich.

2 **Czechoslovakia** had been granted the vital area of the Sudetenland as an important strategic region which provided a defensible mountainous border but fatally contained a German-speaking population. The Czech army and arms industry were strong and represented a significant obstacle to Hitler's ambition. The surrender at Munich deprived the Czechs of the means to defend themselves. It was easy for Hitler to follow up and partition the country in 1939.

3 Hitler understandably played on the principle of national self-determination as he had done successfully in 1936 when Germany re-militarised the Rhineland without opposition. As he was to do in Poland, Hitler used propaganda and employed local Nazis to create problems and excuses for Nazi intervention in **Sudetenland**.

4 After the destruction of the German Communist Party in 1933, Stalin fully realised the threat posed by Fascism. The USSR moved to join the League of Nations and encouraged the formation of anti-fascist "**Popular Front**" governments made up of Socialist, Communist and Liberal coalitions in Spain and France (1936). When the Western Allies failed to confront Fascism in the

Spanish Civil War and gave in at Munich, Stalin sought to buy off Hitler, at least until the USSR could prepare for war.

5 The invasion of **Prague** was the first blatant act of conquest by Hitler. There was no excuse and Chamberlain felt betrayed and humiliated. He moved swiftly to guarantee Poland, Greece and Romania against Nazi attack.

6/7 Hitler was morally unconvincing regarding **Danzig** and the **Polish Corridor** because of the unmasked nature of his aggression over Prague which undermined the genuine grievance regarding German speakers trapped under Polish and League sovereignty. The deal concluded with the USSR, to partition Poland, merely underlined the cynical aggression which, astonishingly, Hitler still thought would not provoke decisive reaction from the Allies.

8 Britain and France were overstretched in Asia. Both were weakened by the Depression, and were intimidated by the apparent strength of the German, Italian and Japanese forces which were technically allied in the Axis agreements. Although the Japanese brought the USA into the war at Pearl Harbor, and Hitler obligingly joined in, the circumstances of the war in the Atlantic made America's entry into the war with Germany quite likely after summer **1941**. Given that Japan had invaded mainland China as early as 1936, some historians feel that the world conflict long preceded 1941.

✔ *Now learn how to use your knowledge*

The coming of World War Two

Use your knowledge

20 minutes

1 Why did the USSR and the Fascist powers get involved in the Spanish Civil War and why did the Allies abstain?

 Hint 1

2 What made China so vulnerable to Japanese attack during the 1930s?

 Hint 2

3 Was the military threat of the Axis powers overestimated by the Allies after 1935 and, if so, why?

Hint 3

4 Why did Italy join the war in June 1940, and Japan join in December 1941?

 Hint 4

Hints and answers follow

The coming of World War Two

Hints

1 The USSR and the Fascists were strongly motivated (for differing reasons) to get involved. The Allies and the USA had strong reasons to keep out.

2 The internal situation of China was extremely disturbed, and had been ever since the collapse of the Manchu dynasty before World War One. China was not immune to ideological struggles similar to those in Europe.

3 Think propaganda, diplomacy and ideology.

4 Look closely at both the ideology and diplomacy of Italy and Japan, and then at the actual military situation in June 1940 and December 1941.

The coming of World War Two

Answers

1 For many anti-Fascist volunteers who joined the International brigades to defend the Spanish Republic against Franco's rebels, the crusade against Fascism which marked World War Two began early. However, France, run by a Popular Front government, was afraid to help its friends in Spain for fear of provoking a similar civil war in France. Britain felt over-stretched and under-armed and was too deeply anti-Communist to trust either the left wing Spanish Republicans or the Russian Communists who were helping them. Both were glad to accept the League of Nations' and the USA's argument that a civil war was an internal affair with which it was illegal to get involved. The Germans and Italians, who were outside the League, were only too happy to ignore this argument and help Franco, their fellow Fascist. It also provided an opportunity to try out new military tactics and weapons. For Stalin and Russia, anti-Fascist ideology, exemplified by the Popular Front policy, demanded action to help the Republicans against Franco.

2 The huge population and potential market of China had been tempting the Western powers since the late nineteenth century. Although the USA claimed to be anti-imperialist, the Americans coveted the Chinese trade. Japan had been militarily active in Korea and Manchuria before World War One and was under pressure from economic depression from the late 1920s onward. By then not only were warlords tearing China apart, but the Chinese Revolution had left the Republicans under Chiang Kai Shek fighting for control against the warlords and against the Communists under Mao Zedong.

3 Fascist propaganda very convincingly played up the power of the Axis troops. Not only did the German propaganda expert, Goebbels convince the British of the huge (and illusory) strength of the *Luftwaffe* (German air force), but Mussolini's propagandists seem to have convinced the dictator himself that he had an army of two million men! Fascist ideology, of course, constantly emphasised the virtues and pleasures of military aggression so the Allies tended to take them at their word, especially as Axis diplomacy was usually made up of violent threats which the Allies could not afford not to take seriously.

4 Italy had been an ally of Nazi Germany since 1935. The Italians had been militarily aggressive in Libya, Abyssinia and, in 1938, in Albania. In theory Mussolini should have joined his ally in declaring war in September 1939, when the Germans invaded Poland. Mussolini only overcame his caution in June 1940 because the war seemed to be about to end. France was on the verge of defeat and Mussolini wanted to cash in at any future peace conference. He therefore invaded the south of France.

Meanwhile, Japan faced a hard choice in 1941. She had invaded Indochina (modern day Vietnam) and an angry USA blocked oil supplies to Japan conditional on Japanese withdrawal. Japan could retreat, and lose face before the Americans, or she could seek alternative oil supplies by attacking the Dutch East Indies (modern Indonesia). This would lead to war with the Netherlands and her ally Britain, and the danger of war with the USA. Having chosen this option, the Japanese decided to pre-empt the risk of war with the USA by knocking out the American fleet at the Pacific base of Pearl Harbor. Japan made this dangerous choice encouraged, no doubt, by the state of the war in December 1941, in which her Axis allies seemed on the verge of victory in Russia and North Africa.

The Cold War

10 minutes

Test your knowledge

The Grand Alliance against Nazi Germany in World War Two was always under strain. Britain and the USA had fought to suppress the Russian Communists in 1917–21 and America had endured a Red Scare in those years.

Nevertheless, at **1** Bronte in March 1945, the Western powers had given Stalin significant concessions in Eastern Europe. The West hoped for Soviet help if an invasion of Japan was necessary, but once Germany was defeated in May 1945 the Allies began to fall out. Tension rose in **2**................. which the Russians had occupied at the end of the war. Meanwhile, no Russian help was needed against Japan because the USA had developed and used the **3**................. .... in August 1945.

Much of Eastern Europe had been occupied by Soviet troops, and when Poland and Czechoslovakia, in particular, fell to Communist governments, the West felt that Russia was breaking the spirit of the wartime agreements. Communist advances in France and Italy, and Communist insurgencies in Greece and Turkey led to the announcement of the **4**................. .... and the development of **5**................. .... to shore up the economies of Western Europe. This help was refused in the Eastern bloc.

The West drew a line in the winter of 1948–9 by using an airlift to defeat the **6**................. .... The sudden fall of China and the Soviet detonation of an A bomb in 1949 and an H bomb in 1951 shocked and frightened the West. **7**................. led to the blacklisting and ruin of alleged left-wingers in the USA and a major war broke out in **8**................. . A partner of indirect and proxy conflict had been set between the super-powers which would persist till 1989.

Answers

1 Yalta 2 Berlin 3 atom/nuclear bomb 4 Truman Doctrine 5 Marshall Aid 6 Berlin Blockade 7 McCarthyism 8 Korea

 If you got them all right, skip to page 59

The Cold War

30 minutes

Improve your knowledge

1 **Yalta** was the penultimate of the wartime allied conferences. It dealt mainly with the settlement of post-war Europe. Allegedly F. D. Roosevelt was too ill to withstand Stalin's demands, and certainly his successor, Harry S. Truman, took a tougher line. Also, by the Potsdam Conference in July, the West had the bomb and were anxious to restrict Russia.

2 The Russians took inevitably high casualties to capture **Berlin**. They spent the early occupation trying to take over all zones of the city but were stopped by German democrats such as Willy Brandt and Konrad Adenauer. Reluctantly the Russians had to admit the Americans, French and British to their respective zones.

3 The **nuclear bomb** gave America a lead which was expected to last at least five years. The rapid Russian development of nuclear technology, helped by the work of the "atom spies" was a shock. Significantly, Russia hurriedly declared war against Japan at the beginning of August 1945 and rushed to advance into Asia to stake out a position for the post-war settlement. This helped make both the Korean and Vietnamese conflicts more likely.

4 Truman had been horrified at the pre-war Allied policy of appeasement and was determined to stand up to any Soviet intimidation. The **Truman Doctrine** in March 1947 promised that the USA "would support free peoples who are resisting subjugation by armed minorities or by outside pressures". Triggered by British inability to hold the line in Greece, it was followed by aid to Greece and Turkey, and also money to secure upcoming elections in Italy and the advance of Communist trade unions in France. It signalled the end of American "isolationist" policies.

5 The Marshall Plan reflected the strength of the US economy and offered huge sums to enable the war-shattered economies of Europe to rebuild and, by generating prosperity, to reject the appeal of Communism. Czechoslovakia showed interest in receiving **Marshall Aid** but was blocked by Russia.

The Soviet system was as much dependent upon creating a self-contained economic bloc as it was in maintaining a repressive political system.

6 West Berlin, as an oasis of Western democracy and economic success deep within the Communist zone, was both a nest of spies for both sides and a constant challenge to the Soviets. The **Berlin Blockade** was an attempt to starve the city into submission and the Allied airlift signalled the West's determination to use all resources to defend Berlin. Thereafter, it was accepted by both sides that Berlin would act as the trigger for general war. Any Russian invasion would be followed by conflict with the considerable Allied forces camped permanently on the plain of West Germany. Both sides, finding Europe too dangerous a site for confrontation, looked elsewhere to compete.

7 The "Red Scare", launched by Senator Joe **McCarthy**, dominated US politics for some years and helped pressure Truman into the Korean War, a costly and ultimately stalemated conflict. Given the suddenness of the fall of China, the development of the Soviet bomb, and the shocking performance of the Western secret services, the level of panic is perhaps understandable.

8 Nevertheless, Truman restricted his anti-Soviet policy to one of "containment", resisting the advance of Communism into South Korea. After some hesitation he resisted his Commander, Douglas MacArthur's attempt to "roll-back" Communism by invading North **Korea** and China. MacArthur was dismissed but Truman's successors continued to be drawn into conflicts of containment for the rest of the Cold War. The beginning of the Korean War also highlighted the failings of the United Nations. Up to 1950, Russia and America had respectively blocked each other's initiatives by using their veto powers in the Security Council. Because the Russian delegates were boycotting the UN in 1950, Truman was able to condemn the Communist invasion of South Korea and to set up a counter-attack under the banner of the United Nations. In contrast to the pre-War League of Nations, at least this ensured that the UN would, in future, be able to deploy force in international disputes.

✔ *Now learn how to use your knowledge*

The Cold War

Use *your knowledge*

30 minutes

1 Why were the fates of Czechoslovakia and Poland especially important?

2 In what ways might a "Red Scare" with its fear of spies and traitors cause harm to the ideals and living standards of Western democracies such as Britain and the USA?

3 Define the main principles dividing the Soviet bloc and the so-called "Free World" or Western democracies.

4 In what ways did the Soviet development of a rival nuclear bomb affect the course and nature of the Cold War?

5 The West can claim to have "won" the Cold War. Suggest reasons for this victory.

Hints and answers follow

The Cold War

1 Think about pre-war policies of appeasement.

2 The West stood for (or claimed to) important freedoms of the individual, of speech, assembly, opinion and for fair systems of justice. How might these freedoms be affected by the panic about Communism?

3 See Hint 2 but also note that the USSR often claimed to support certain kinds of nationalism.

4 Think arms race, economics and deterrence.

5 There is both a "moral" answer, about freedoms and values, and a material argument about the economies of the rival superpowers.

The Cold War

Answers

1 The West, much influenced by Churchill's warnings of the 1930s and his wartime career, was influenced by the perceived betrayals of appeasement. Churchill's criticisms of the appeasers were vindicated by his success. The West had been particularly ashamed of its weakness in "betraying" Czechoslovakia at Munich in 1938. Moreover, Britain and France had gone to war in 1939 to **save** Poland. The loss of both countries to Stalin's brutal Communist regimes caused great anguish.

2 Red Scares tend to lead to attacks on freedom of speech and of the Press. Under McCarthy, many innocent people were rushed before crude and very biased trials before the Senate committee, and liberals and intellectuals were often unfairly persecuted. In short, the freedom of an individual to hold personal political opinions came very much under attack.

3 The "Free World" genuinely did argue for an emphasis on individual freedoms, within a free economic world where most economies were subject to all the advantages and disadvantages of freedom, i.e. flexible wages (high or low), consumer choice and more and better goods, but with the dangers of unemployment, homelessness and so on. The Eastern bloc emphasised equality rather than liberty and played on such workers' rights as the right to a job and the right to accommodation. Although quite brutal towards national revolts and movements in Europe, where East Germans, Poles, Hungarians and Czechs all suffered violently during the Cold War, the Soviets did support many national liberation movements around the world. The resistance of old imperial powers like Britain, France and Portugal to the movements for independence and decolonisation in Africa and Asia and the many peasant revolts in Latin America, played into Soviet hands. They could claim to stand for freedom from "Western Imperialism".

4 Nuclear rivalry changed everything. The threat of "Mutually Assured Destruction" created the concept of Nuclear Deterrence, i.e. that both superpowers would be sincerely terrified of starting a nuclear war that would assure they themselves suffered unacceptable damage, whatever the outcome. However, once that level of weaponry was achieved, an Arms Race continued to spiral, while both sides tried to prevent proliferation, as other countries tried to join the nuclear club. For most of the Cold War, only the superpowers and China acquired significant nuclear arsenals. The Arms Race, meanwhile was a contest to decide the merits of two rival economic systems, hence the intense "Space Age" rivalry and the US determination to put a man on the Moon. USSR successes in the 1950s with Sputnik boosted Soviet confidence. "We will bury you", boasted Khrushchev. As late as 1979, Nicaragua, Iran, Grenada and Afghanistan all fell out from American or under Soviet influence and Western leaders were alarmed and increased their arms spending and research. Meanwhile, from the first Soviet bomb, it became clearly too dangerous for US and Soviet troops to meet directly in battle. Both sides fought "proxy" wars "under the nuclear umbrella" as Henry Kissinger said. Russians fought Afghans armed by America while US marines fought the Viet Cong who were supplied, armed and encouraged by China and Russia. More often, forces armed by either side demonstrated the superiority or inferiority of Western or Eastern technology in their local struggles. Hence the US triumph when its technology, wielded by Israel, crushed the Soviet-equipped Syrian airforce in 1973.

5 The moral argument is quite strong. The Eastern bloc did systematically restrict individual rights and freedoms and did blatantly use Secret Police, torture and, under Stalin, massacre and concentration-style camps. Although the dubious activities of certain Western agencies, and certain unpleasant allies tarnished many Western efforts, as did aspects of the war effort in Vietnam, nevertheless the West probably stood for more attractive values.

The material argument is more straightforward. The Soviet bloc economy, despite the flashy successes of the Sputnik era, and its very real military achievement, could not produce attractive Western standards of living. Decent food, pleasant housing and choice or even supply of consumer goods were sacrificed in order to produce the rockets, tanks and spaceships. It is doubtful if a state-organised economy could have succeeded, even without the Arms Race. Although the huge arms spending under President Reagan and his allies did force the creaking Soviet system into an economic contest it simply could not win, and which would ruin it, it is possible that the proximity of Western standards of living, clearly visible on Western TV stations finally drove neighbouring East Germans, Poles, Hungarians and Czechs to defy the system in the 1980s.

The Arab–Israeli conflict

10 minutes

Test your knowledge

As an act of deliberate **1**................... , Hitler and the Nazis organised the elaborate murder of at least six million Jews during World War Two. After the war, the newly formed United Nations, the British, who were mandate holders for **2**................... , and the USA felt that the long-sought Jewish homeland should be situated in the Middle East from which the people originated but from which they had scattered in the **3**................... since the Roman conquest in the first century AD.

There was already a powerful **4**................... movement which had long campaigned for such a homeland. Thousands of Jewish refugees of Nazism now fled to their hoped-for homeland. Nationalist groups used terror against the British authorities, notably **5**................... and the **6**................... ....
7................... , a senior UN official, was murdered and the King David Hotel bombed. The UN and the great powers brokered an agreement, but on independence the neighbouring Arab powers attempted to crush the new state at birth, while the Israelis drove out refugees through military victories and systematic intimidation. Improvised refugee camps provided a fertile recruiting ground for "freedom fighters", the so-called **8**................... , who fought guerrilla actions in the 1950s against the new state.

After Arab defeats in the **9**................... ....
in 1967, which increased the refugee problem, political terrorism led by the **10**.
.... took a high profile with murders, notably at the
11................... .... in 1972 and through **12**................... .
Further wars took place in 1973 and in the **13**................... in 1982.
UN Resolution No. **14**................... , the **15**................... ....
agreements, and international responses to the **16**................... led to faltering attempts at lasting agreement during the 1990s.

Answers

1 genocide 2 Palestine 3 Diaspora 4 Zionist 5 Irgun
6 Stern Gang 7 Bernadotte 8 Fedayeen 9 Six Day
War 10 PLO (Palestine Liberation Organization)
11 Munich Olympics 12 Hijacking 13 Lebanon
14 242 15 Camp David 16 Intifada

 If you got them all right, skip to page 67

63

The Arab–Israeli conflict

Improve your knowledge

20 minutes

1 In the twentieth century a new word had to be coined to describe the systematic murder of people on account of their race. The first example was probably the extermination of millions of Armenians by the Turks during World War One. The "Shoah" or "Holocaust" featured a combination of mass shootings, the working to death and starvation of inmates of work camps such as Auschwitz, and the use of gas chambers to wipe out the victims of Hitler's and the Nazis' obsessive anti-semitism. Since World War Two the mutual **genocide** of Hutus and Tutsis in Rwanda–Burundi and of Serbs, Bosnians, Croatians and Muslims in the former Yugoslavia indicate that genocide still thrives.

2 **Palestine** fell under British supervision after the defeat of the Ottoman empire in World War One. Famously, different British authorities made different promises to the Jews (Balfour Declaration) and the Arabs (Lawrence of Arabia). Even before World War Two there was violence, terrorism and discontent within the mandate.

3 **Diaspora** means the dispersal of a people. After the Roman conquest, |Jews dispersed all over Europe and the Middle East, attracting prejudice in Christian countries for their peoples' role in the rejection of Christ, and by the perceived alienness of their culture and beliefs. Ironically the troubles of their enemies since 1947 has led to a distinctive Palestinian diaspora around the world.

4 The **Zionist** movement, rejuvenated by Theodor Herzl (1860–1904), obtained the Balfour Declaration (1917) and triumphantly secured the Middle Eastern homeland in 1948. Extreme Zionists demand an "*Eretz Israel* which would comprehend the boundaries of the Jewish empire under the biblical King David" – not an aim conducive to lasting or likely Middle Eastern peace.

5-7 Like many nationalist movements before or since, the Israelis, partly inspired by the passive and victim image created by the Holocaust, took an active terrorist role. Fighters such as Moshe Dyan and Menachem Begin later became respected international statesmen and political leaders of their country. Famous actions carried out by **Irgun** and **The Stern Gang**, included the murder of **Bernadotte**, the bombing of the King David Hotel, and the massacres in the Arab village of Deir Yassin in 1947 which helped precipitate the flight of Palestinian refugees.

8 **Fedayeen** were early examples of Arab "freedom fighters", responsible for raids across the Israeli borders from refugee camps in the Lebanon and Jordan.

9 President Abdel Nasser was the hero of Arab nationalism who had successfully defied the British and French in the Suez Crisis of 1956, briefly created the United Arab Republic of Syria and Egypt (1958–61), and, with Soviet help, had built up a significant Egyptian army and airforce. Allegedly provoked into a premature attack upon Israel in 1967, the destruction of Egyptian air power left his land forces open to destruction in a swift and inglorious campaign. Israeli gains in the **Six Day War**, especially in Sinai, the Gaza Strip and on the West Bank compounded an already grim refugee problem, and left a desperate Palestinian nationalist movement with few aggressive options other than terrorism.

10-12 The **PLO** remains the representative of the Palestinian people, under the leadership of Yasser Arafat, as recognised by the UN General Assembly since 1974. Because of the Cold War they generally derived military and diplomatic support from the USSR, while the USA and the West tended to back Israel, although the UK have always retained sentimental links with remnants of Arab elements in the former British Empire. Although increasingly moderate, the PLO have long been outbid by its fighting element, Al Fatah, by the Palestinian Liberation Army, and Arab movements such as Hamas. The killings at the **Munich Olympics** for example, were carried out by the Black September offshoot, made up of angry Palestinians driven out of Jordan by King Hussein in 1971. **Hijacking** of airliners was a modern and dramatic way of obtaining international recognition for a cause. Such techniques were taken up by other groups in the 1960s and 1970s such as the Baader–Meinhoff group and the Red Army Faction. Assassinations, bombings and suicide tactics are variations which have persisted to the present day.

13 The invasion of the **Lebanon** was the first overtly aggressive war undertaken by Israel, in order to expel the PLO from bases among the Lebanese refugee camps. Civilian bombings and general aggression and clumsiness united various Lebanese factions against the Israelis whose forces became embroiled in a bloody and unpopular stalemate. This action increased recognition of the Palestinian and Arab case while the contemporary Iranian revolution increased awareness in the West of the significant power of Islamic Fundamentalism which greatly reinforced the morale and level of anti-Israeli and anti-Western terrorist activity.

14 Originally, **Resolution 242** was passed because of the strong support of Arabs and ex-colonial countries in the UN assembly, backed by Soviet sympathy arising from Cold War rivalry with US support of Israel. Increasingly, UN support became more obviously principled and difficult for the West and Israel to resist.

15 After Nasser's death in 1970 his successor as ruler of Egypt, Anwar Sadat, confronted Israel in the Yom Kippur War of 1973. He was defeated and switched allegiance to the West and opened negotiations with Israel which were brokered by American President Jimmy Carter, resulting in the **Camp David** peace agreement in which Menachem Begin of Israel traded peace for land, handing Sinai back to the Egyptians. Sadat's pro-Western policies led to his assassination by Islamic fundamentalists in 1981, but his successor, Hosni Mubarak, has kept Egypt generally in the Western camp ever since.

16 Over many years Israel traded successfully as a David figure against the Goliath image of the hostile surrounding Arab nations. The aggression in the Lebanon was followed by the *Intifada* in which Palestinian children and youths took up resistance against Israeli occupation of the West Bank and the Gaza Strip by a combination of passive resistance, stone-throwing and demonstrations which subverted this image. Shootings and repression gravely damaged Israel's international reputation and helped lead to the post-1990 Peace Process.

✔ *Now learn how to use your knowledge*

The Arab–Israeli conflict

Use your knowledge

20 minutes

1 What was the Suez Crisis of 1956 and why was it important?

Hint 1

2 Why is the West careful to remain friendly with several major Arab countries in the Middle Eastern region?

Hint 2

3 What links do the French, British and the USA have in the region? Why are these important?

Hint 3

4 Briefly, what is the significance of Jerusalem for three major world religions?

Hint 4

5 Four Arab or Persian leaders; President Nasser of Egypt, President Saddam Hussein of Iraq, Yasser Arafat of Palestine, Ayatollah Khomeini of Iran. What similarities and what differences can be found in their appeal to Arab nationalists?

Hint 5

✔ **Hints and answers follow**

The Arab–Israeli conflict

Hints

1 Britain had long occupied Egypt, and France had long possessed business interests there. Think hard about Israel's and America's interests at the time.

2 Oil and what else?

3 Follows on from questions 1 and 2, but think about World War One, and about earlier questions of Empire.

4 The three are Christian, Muslim and Jewish.

5 Consider their rejection or acceptance of Westernisation; Fundamentalism or otherwise in religion.

Answers

1 Colonel, later President Nasser, helped win Egyptian independence from the British Empire. He accepted Soviet money and support and nationalised the Suez Canal, which provoked a co-ordinated attack by Britain, France and Israel who occupied the Canal zone and Sinai. The USA forced the Allies to retreat and Israel to give up Sinai. It provided Israel with another clear military success, humiliated England and France and made it clear they could no longer easily act independently of America.

More significantly, it brought the USSR to pose as a supporter of Arab nationalism and, in the long term, established the USA as Israel's staunchest ally.

2 Oil is obviously important and is produced notably by the Arab states, and by Iran and Iraq. These states provide huge business opportunities, particularly in arms sales, while several, e.g. Saudi Arabia and Iran before 1979, were clearly useful allies against the Soviet bloc.

3 Both Britain and France were Mediterranean powers with trading and territorial links. Both fought against the Ottoman Empire during the war and obtained important Middle Eastern mandates (Palestine and Jordan in Britain's case while France was given Syria and the Lebanon). Oil, trade and strategy mean they remain involved in the present day. The USA gradually became sucked in because of the Cold War, and after 1971 when she became a net importer of oil.

4 Jerusalem is fundamentally the site of Christ's Passion and Crucifixion. Long before then it had been a Holy City to the Jews and the site of the great Temple which was sacked by the Romans. In the seventh century AD Mohammed founded the Islamic

Revolution, sparked the Muslim conquest of much of the Middle East and Mediterranean region and chose to ascend to Paradise from Jerusalem.

5 Nasser was a Westernised military man who accepted Soviet aid for his Pan–Arab Nationalism. Saddam Hussein of Iraq was originally a client of the West, who fell out with them and acquired his role as Arab leader accidentally, though playing it up in his assault on Israel during the Gulf War. Arafat as PLO leader represents thousands of Palestinian Christian Arabs as well as Muslims, and is recognisably a Western and rather secular figure in uniform, culture and religion which has at times meant he has been easily outbid by religious fundamentalists. The Persian Khomeini was an inspiration to millions of extremely fundamentalist Muslims in Iran and elsewhere, who reject the West, its culture, religion and influence.

Despite Nasser's best efforts, Arabs and Palestinians have rarely achieved a united front due to tribal, nationalist and religious differences and local rivalries.

10 minutes

Test your knowledge

The Communist party of China (CCP) came close to elimination at the hands of Chiang Kai Shek's **1**................. . However, in 1934, the Communists, led by Mao Zedong, undertook the **2**................. .... over a whole year, to the remote Yunnan province. Gradually, Mao perfected the tactics of guerrilla war, converting China's peasants to his cause.

During the war, the Communists fought as patriots and by 1945 were ready to compete for power. The USA and her allies backed Chiang. Despite this, the CCP triumphed in 1949. Signing a long-term treaty to gain Soviet aid, the Chinese fought with some success in the Korean war, invaded **3**................. and clashed with India over **4**................. .

Meanwhile, after **5**................. agriculture and exterminating the landlords, Mao lost faith in Soviet methods and opted for the **6**................. .... campaign in 1957 followed by the ambitious **7**................. .... from 1958 to 1961. This led to famine and disastrous loss of life, and Mao went temporarily into eclipse. A struggle between himself and the so-called "rightists" was resolved in 1966 by the **8**................. .... which attempted the radical renewal of revolutionary attitudes in the party, spearheaded by the young **9**................. ...., and imprisoned, murdered and "re-educated" alleged counter revolutionaries. After Mao's death in 1976 the power struggle involving the **10**................. .... was followed, after 1978, by the rise of **11**................. .... , under whose leadership China moved towards economic reform. Incentives were introduced and overtures from the West, which had been spearheaded by **12**................. .... of the USA in 1972, were followed up. However, protests and pro-democracy demands were brutally crushed at **13**................. .... in 1989.

Answers

1 Kuomintang (KMT, sometimes known as the Nationalists) **2** Long March **3** Tibet **4** Kashmir **5** collectivising **6** Hundred Flowers **7** Great Leap Forward **8** Cultural Revolution **9** Red Guards **10** Gang of Four **11** Deng Xiao Ping **12** Richard Nixon **13** Tiananmen Square.

 If you got them all right, skip to page 75

20
minutes

Improve *your knowledge*

1 Although the Chinese Revolution of 1911 toppled the Manchu Empire, Sun Yat Sen failed to establish a stable Republic as China fell apart among various warlords. Chiang Kai Shek and his **KMT** claimed to represent Sun's ideals (he died in 1925) but Chiang's corruption and increasingly dictatorial style rather resembled that of contemporary Fascists.

2 The epic **Long March** played a great part in Mao's legend and leadership and saved the Communists who were able to regroup and relaunch themselves. The chief lesson learned was to avoid the cities where the strong Communist presence of the 1920s had been easily identified and wiped out by the KMT. The latter were strong in the towns and buoyed up by US aid. They fatally underestimated the Communists' almost total control of the countryside, which enabled their armies to capture the key cities of China in the short but ferocious campaigns of 1949, driving the KMT into exile in Taiwan (formerly Formosa).

3 Claimed and invaded by the Chinese in 1949–50, **Tibet** has been occupied, its spiritual and political leader, the Dalai Lama, driven into exile, and subjected to a systematic colonisation ever since.

4 This brief war took place in 1962. India, after several humiliating reverses, was relieved when the Chinese abandoned their advance. China has since been relatively friendly to India, although happy to exploit the rivalry with neighbouring Pakistan, not least over **Kashmir**.

5 The CCP reversed the methods of the Bolshevik revolution. Where the Bolsheviks seized the town and then conquered the countryside in the Civil War, the CCP had already virtually occupied the rural areas before finally toppling the KMT posts in the towns in 1949. Unlike the Soviets, who waited to recover from the civil war for most of a decade, the CCP immediately took over the land and redistributed it to the peasants in **collective farms** while eliminating or re-educating the landlords.

6 The **Hundred Flowers** campaign aimed to encourage constructive criticism and debate between the new industrial workers and technicians in China and the party "cadres" (the groups of party officials who directed and organised the Chinese masses). It backfired when the cadres and the party itself were deluged with angry criticism and demands for greater freedom of discussion and organisation. Mao clamped down.

7 The **Great Leap Forward** arose partly from Mao's reaction to the Hundred Flowers criticism. Rejecting Soviet advice to continue organising industry along the lines of the Soviet Five Year Plans, Mao envisaged backyard steel mills and de-centralisation of production accompanied by massive programmes of public works on roads, dams, bridges etc. The simultaneous setting up of huge communes added to chaos and disaster. Although millions died, some historians argue that the campaign laid the long-term foundations for more efficient running of Chinese agriculture and industry.

8 During the worst years of the Great Leap Forward, Mao's influence was under threat from Rightists like Deng Xiao Ping who proposed dilution of Communist methods by capitalist techniques such as incentives. The **Cultural Revolution** was both Mao's struggle to retain personal leadership against his enemies, and a massive and largely successful attempt to refocus the CCP as a pure Communist party and government, purging the party of foreign and moderate influences.

9 The **Red Guards**, many of them mere schoolchildren, were ideal shock-troops, willing to attack their parents' generation and humiliate and brutalise all who were seen as tainted by faintheartedness or Westernisation. They fulfilled Mao's schemes for power and for purging the party but rampaged out of control for some years after the initial campaign had achieved its objects.

10 The **Gang of Four** included Mao's wife. This group were fanatical Marxists whose policies were too extreme to be acceptable in a party recovering from the worst years of the Cultural Revolution and in which former Rightists were beginning to return to influence.

11 Despite exile and ill-treatment during the Cultural Revolution, **Deng Xiao Ping** survived and returned to lead the group of old Communists who directed China into the 1990s. The same generation as Mao allowed corruption and economic flexibility but remained terrified of political freedom.

12 **Richard Nixon**'s greatest foreign policy success was his visit to China in 1972. Despite mutual political suspicion, both were anxious to obtain economic benefits and to open potentially profitable trade links.

13 Since Nixon's mission, China had steadily opened up its trade to the rest of the world and introduced incentives and profit techniques into its industry and agriculture. Such reform predictably sparked demands among the younger generations of Chinese for meaningful political and social freedoms. Encouraged by the Western media, lengthy student pro-democracy demonstrations in Beijing got out of hand in the summer of 1989. Deng's regime allowed hardliners to direct the Army in a brutal massacre to disperse the protests. The violence, the blatant nature of the **Tiananmen Square** clamp down and the heavy casualties (perhaps 3 000) exposed the regime temporarily to a torrent of criticism, but by the early 1990s Western interest in the Chinese economy led to a restoration of trade and economic relations. Even after Deng's death no meaningful political change occurred.

✔ *Now learn how to use your knowledge*

20 minutes

Use your knowledge

1 Why were the CCP able to defeat the KMT and take power in China in 1949? **Hint ❶**

2 Account for the Sino–Soviet split. **Hint ❷**

3 Why was Mao able to hold power until his death in 1976? **Hint ❸**

4 In what ways were the Great Leap Forward and the Cultural Revolution successes, and in what ways failures? **Hint ❹**

5 Account for the lack of political reform in China since Mao's death. **Hint ❺**

6 How far have China's relations with the rest of the world improved since Mao's death? **Hint ❻**

✔ Hints and answers follow

Hints

1 Look at the CCP's strengths and the KMT's weaknesses (and vice versa). Stress the importance of the peasants in a mainly rural country.

2 Look at what the two sides had in common, and their differences in culture, economy and ambition. What reasons might make them stick together? What pushed them apart?

3 What makes a successful dictator? Think Hitler, Stalin, Mussolini – what techniques did they have in common?

4 Learn to define what you mean by success. What kind of failures did not worry Mao and his party? What were their priorities?

5 This again, is about Chinese, or CCP, priorities, and perhaps, about outside pressure.

6 Some clear ups and downs to think of, e.g. war with Vietnam in 1979, embarrassment over Tiananmen Square. What policies have been consistent since 1976?

Answers

1 Standard answers refer to corruption and incompetence within the KMT resulting in poor morale and poor performance from KMT troops. The Nationalists put up an indifferent performance against the Japanese, whereas the CCP appeared united and patriotic. The persistence of class differences and antagonism among the KMT officers and ranks also affected military performance.

Mao's appeal to the peasants was crucial. It was not possible, as in Russia in 1917, to capture key cities and dominate China in the same way. There was not enough industry to paralyse the country the way the Bolsheviks did in 1917, while the use of guerrilla methods made it impossible to identify and eliminate the Communist cadres. Because the Communists were immersed among the peasantry, attacks upon them simply drove Communists and peasants closer together. Again, class was crucial. Ultimately the KMT seemed too close to the interests of the landlords. Worse, in accepting American aid they lost credibility as patriots. Finally, Mao imposed the kind of party discipline, copied from Lenin and Stalin, that provided a unity of purpose that the Nationalists could not match.

2 Soviets and CCP had a basic common interest as the first two Communist parties to seize power in the modern world. They shared a common isolation and a natural resentment against the "Capitalist" powers who were openly hostile, in turn, to them. Natural respect towards the Soviets as the pioneers of world revolution could, however, veer into resentment due to patronising Soviet attitudes, grudging aid, and outright refusal to share Soviet nuclear secrets with China. Soviet insistence that theirs was the "right" road to "Socialism" was palpably wrong given the different conditions in China. Russian and Chinese nationalism and culture naturally enough divided them. Mao's personal contempt for the undignified Khrushchev as Soviet leader after the revered Stalin deepened divisions. Russia found herself cast into the role of alarmed elder power trying to rein in a more extreme, brash and aggressive younger revolutionary power.

3 Like many successful twentieth-century dictators, Mao played heavily upon the cult of personality. First he polished the myths associated with the Long March and the struggles against the Japanese and in the Civil War. Later, particularly in the Cultural Revolution, he played up the cult of the Little Red Book and of the all-wise Chairman. Like Lenin, Stalin and Hitler, he was skilled at the art of "divide and rule" using disputes over future policy to isolate and expose his personal opponents. The repeated dramatic campaigns to purge the party and rekindle revolutionary spirit were well calculated to pick out and defeat opponents and rivals.

4 Given China's immense population, mass casualties were acceptable in the same way as Stalin's collectivisation and five year plans were only inefficient in Western terms. The brutal mobilisation and the subjection to discipline of millions of unfortunates was doubly efficient. It got things done, no matter how clumsily or bloodily, and it kept the masses under control. Even the famines caused by the Great Leap Forward weakened possible resistance. The campaigns were largely about strengthening the Party elite, and specifically Mao's control over the country, and in this respect they succeeded.

5 Following on from question 4, political control for the Party at all levels is essential. Peasants, provinces, successful profit-making businessmen, and army leaders are subject, ultimately, to Party control. In 1989 the army revealed that it was still a reliable tool of last resort in maintaining that control. There have been protests from international pressure groups such as Amnesty International, and significant speeches by British prime ministers and American presidents, but the old generation certainly maintained control up to Deng's death. It is possible that the generation born since the Civil War may be more flexible about political change, having accepted considerable economic liberalism. They will, however, be horribly aware of the dangers of revolt, chaos and loss of control.

6 Since Mao's death the Chinese showed open enmity (dating back for centuries) towards their Vietnamese neighbours. Support for them against America in the 1960s had been a matter of Communist belief and sheer opportunism. Since 1972 a simple pro-Western approach based on economic needs and trade openings, without yielding anything much on political rights, has only marginally been affected by the Tiananmen affair. The Chinese have been able to let dislike of their Russian neighbours be more obvious since the collapse of the Soviet system.

South Africa and apartheid

10 minutes

Test your knowledge

South Africa was made up of two largely British-dominated provinces, Natal and the Cape, together with the **1**................... and **2**................... .... which were occupied by the **3**................... , a people of Dutch extraction who had always practised a form of "apartheid" upon non-whites. There were many non-whites, including Asian labourers, the **4**................... .... of mixed race, and the **5**................... . When the National Party won the 1948 elections, apartheid was extended to the whole country. Attempts were made to completely separate the different communities, although, of course non-whites were needed to work in industry and to act as servants. Therefore complicated **6**................... .... were introduced to identify every individual by race and to establish their right to live and work in particular areas. All existing political rights for the African population were abolished, and sexual relations between the races became illegal.

The **7**................... .... – .... set up supposed independent states for the Africans called **8**................... , such as Bophuthatswana and Venda, while townships, such as the famous **9**................... , were set up to house workers needed in the big cities.

African leaders stepped up protests notably at **10**................... in 1960 and **11**................... in 1976. The brutal response to peaceful demonstration led to a direct response by the **12**................... .... whose actions led to the imprisonment of Nelson Mandela (1964). Many others died in secret as victims of police brutality, such as **13**................... .... in 1978. International criticism isolated South Africa and the UN and separate governments introduced **14**................... . Ultimately, economic weaknesses forced the regime to release Mandela and negotiate.

 If you got them all right, skip to page 83

20 minutes

Improve *your knowledge*

1/2 The Boers had occupied the Cape area in the seventeenth century but the Cape fell to the British after the Napoleonic Wars in 1815. Many Boers had disliked British rule and carried out the Great Trek of the 1840s in which they established the two republics of **Transvaal** and the **Orange Free State** after a number of wars with the Zulus and other Bantu tribes who were migrating southwards.

3 The **Boers** speak a form of Dutch known as "Afrikaans" and argued that they were effectively the first owners of much of South Africa as the original bushmen died out and the Bantu were themselves migrants from the north.

4 The theories of separate development came late. Under the race laws, Boers might be embarrassed to trace their families back too many generations as mixed marriages had clearly once been very common in producing the communities of **Cape Coloureds**!

5 **Bantus** were themselves divided into tribal groups and assigned different tribal areas by the apartheid laws. Many Zulus under their leader, Chief Buthelezi, agreed with this principle and became opponents of the ANC.

6 **Pass Laws** were the core of the apartheid system and were picked out for protest by the first great African leader, Albert Luthuli. They were the target of the Sharpeville demonstration, pictures of which shocked international opinion.

7/8 The **Bantu Self-Government Act**, which was responsible for the setting up of the **Bantustans** simply extended the principle of defining race and allocating jobs, accommodation and education accordingly. Ultimately the Bantustans were intended simply as giant reserves of cheap labour for the whites to employ. As they received "independence", they were left somehow to resolve the problems of poverty, high unemployment and dreadful social facilities which the South African government could claim were not legally their concern.

9 Under the Group Areas Act, each community outside the later Bantustans system was allocated separate areas in which to live. **Soweto** itself is a huge sprawling urban region ranging from shanty-town poverty through to the villas of a growing black middle class.

10/11 **Sharpeville** led to the first international action with South Africa leaving the Commonwealth, being ejected in 1964 from the Olympic Games and subject after 1968 to boycotts in cricket and other sports. Consumer boycotts followed and increasingly banks and other major institutions became reluctant to invest. The **Soweto** protests were directed against the low quality of Bantu education, which was deliberately under-financed, and in particular at the decision to enforce the learning of Afrikaans. The Soweto killings gained huge publicity from scenes featured in Richard Attenborough's movie *Cry Freedom*.

12 The **ANC** was partly inept and partly gentlemanly in approach in the 1960s. Later, hardened by the brutality of the South African police and by years of welfare, its members fought from bases in neighbouring Angola and Mozambique and graduated to outright terrorism which earned rebukes from the then British Prime Minister Mrs Thatcher. Mandela's patience and unvengeful demeanour and the patient diplomacy of second-in-command, Oliver Tambo, made the organisation the most important mouthpiece of African resistance to apartheid.

13 **Steve Biko** was a particularly charismatic and effective black consciousness leader active in the 1970s. The circumstances of his death were entirely typical of the fate of hundreds of other unsung victims but were effectively exposed by journalist friends to cause lasting discredit to the increasingly isolated apartheid regime.

14 Sharpeville, Soweto and Biko all brought bad publicity. The sports-mad Boers were hurt by specific boycotts. Spontaneous hard-headed business decisions in the form of **sanctions** in the 1980s seem to have been even more effective, particularly as American investors pulled out from a region seen as a bad risk. As Angola, Mozambique and Zimbabwe gained independence by 1980, South Africa appeared as the isolated site for an imminent race war which would be very bad for business. Business disinvestment underlined the case for compromise.

✔ *Now learn how to use your knowledge*

Use your knowledge

20 minutes

1 Harold Macmillan told South Africans that he had noticed a "wind of change" soon after Sharpeville. Why, therefore, was Mrs Thatcher holding out against sanctions and condemning the ANC as a terrorist organisation as late as 1988?

2 Why was America increasingly inclined to disapprove of South African apartheid after 1965?

3 Why did the strategic case against South Africa seem more compelling after 1989?

4 What ideas seem to have influenced the founders and defenders of apartheid?

5 "Without Nelson Mandela there could have been no peaceful transition to majority rule in South Africa." Discuss.

Hints and answers follow

1 Macmillan shared the general sense of optimism about the decolonisation process that was going on in the 1960s. The ANC was certainly responsible for attacks on civilians. Also think IRA, Libya, Communism etc.

2 Until the mid-1960s the Southern States of America were themselves responsible for a type of apartheid which had to be painfully dismantled by the Civil Rights Movement.

3 The South Africans repeatedly linked black and African nationalist movements with the spread of Communism.

4 Note that South Africa's wartime government was sympathetic to Hitler's ideas and unwilling to give Britain formal support in the war.

5 Mandela had been consistently and remarkably forgiving where others might have been less so. The history of atrocity and counter-atrocity and the particular crimes of the apartheid regime were not an encouraging background.

South Africa and apartheid

Answers

1 In 1960 there was real hope that newly independent states, including those in Africa, were going to develop into prosperous democratic nations, friendly towards their former imperial "masters". Furthermore, although real tensions between West and East (notably over Cuba, 1962) would happen again, 1960 was a time of dialogue and the main advances of Soviet-backed regimes and resistance groups in Africa were a thing of the future. From Mrs Thatcher's perspective of the 1980s there was a "New" Cold War, and the ANC by accepting aid from the Soviets or their clients (Angola and Mozambique were perceived as pro-Soviet) was simply on the wrong side. The USA tended to agree with her. She had also narrowly escaped a terrorist (IRA) bomb in 1984.

2 The USA was, in the Cold War, likely to sympathise with the South African argument that they were a force for anti-Communism. The scenes from Sharpeville were, however, embarrassingly similar to those from the Civil Rights marches down south. As black voters regained their rights in the USA, they were unlikely to vote for open supporters of the apartheid regime. The South Africans were themselves aware of the need for diplomacy and pushed the anti-Communist line while maintaining that the independence of the Bantustans was a liberal move involving giving the inhabitants greater freedom.

3 The collapse of Communism in 1989 with the fall of the Berlin Wall and the end of the East European Communist regimes, removed the whole strategic argument from the South Africans while Soviet aid for African regimes and freedom fighters rapidly tailed off.

4 Apartheid originated from the old religious ideas of a chosen race to be found in the Old Testament. The Boer Dutch Reformed Church developed such ideas back in the nineteenth century, perhaps earlier. However, more modern ideas of racism, which were common in the twentieth century and which also inspired the Nazis, were picked up and became popular in South Africa in the 1930s and 1940s.

5 Mandela, originally a lawyer, lent charisma and coherence to the movement before and after he went to prison. His words at his trial focused his followers, while imprisonment kept his reputation clear from the normal compromises of active politics. He was a symbol while his wife, Winnie, and leaders like Tambo and Archbishop Tutu kept the flame alive. Violent possibilities were ever present. The use of "necklacing" and the motto "one settler, one bullet", which went on in the townships, were rejected by Mandela and after 1989 his vision and reputation undoubtedly inspired many to give peace a chance. Crucially, Prime Minister De Klerk was persuaded, probably rightly, that Mandela was his only chance. The examples of the long civil wars in Angola, Mozambique and Zimbabwe, also acted as a warning to compromise.

The preceding chapters have largely concentrated on the need to check basic knowledge of terminology and understanding of concepts. There have been some documentary passages to analyse and a few visual stimuli in the form of photographs or posters. In exam conditions you will face both passages and pictures which will test not only the above aspects of your knowledge, but will also examine your skills of analysis of the quality of evidence before you. In other words, you need to keep a sharp eye out for the viewpoint, bias and accuracy of evidence. Below is a selection of material and some representative questions.

Example one: Nazi Germany

Source A: A poster issued by the Nazis in 1937.
The caption on the poster reads "Mother and Child".

Source B: Joseph Goebbels, Head of Nazi Propaganda, writing in 1929.

"The mission of women is to be beautiful and to bring children into the world. The female bird pretties herself for her mate and hatches eggs for him. In exchange, the male takes care of gathering the food and stands guard and fights off the enemy."

Source C: Adolf Hitler, commenting on the heavy losses sustained by German soldiers fighting at Stalingrad.

"But that is what the young men are for."

1 How useful are these three sources as evidence about Nazi policy towards women? **(6)**

2 What are the purposes of these three sources? How genuinely do you think they reflect the attitudes of Hitler and the Nazis towards women in general? **(6)**

3 From the above sources and from your own knowledge, give an account of Nazi attitudes towards the role of both genders in the Third Reich. **(8)**

Total marks = 20

Example two: The Arab–Israeli conflict

Source A: Photograph of young heavily armed
Palestinian boys and girls.

Source B: Extract from a speech made by President Nasser at the Egyptian
Advanced Air Headquarters on 22 May 1967.

> "On 13 May we received accurate information that Israel was concentrating
> huge armed forces on the Syrian Border. We told our Syrian brothers that if
> they were attacked Egypt would fight. We had no plan for war before 13 May.
> The Jews threaten war. We tell them you are welcome, we are ready for war."

Source C: During interviews with journalists in August 1967 Abba Eiban,
Israeli Foreign Minister, discusses the war.

> "Israel has no intention of wasting the position won by its war victory and will
> hold land captured from the Arabs until a satisfactory peace is reached. What
> happened in 1967 happened because in 1957 Israel had been persuaded to
> give up the fruits of victory. This time there will be a different map of Israel."

1 How reliable is Source B as an explanation of the outbreak of the Six Day War? In what ways might it be biased? **(6)**

2 How far does Source A confirm the account in Source B of Arab fears of Israeli attack? How might an Israeli commentator view Source A? **(6)**

3 Why might the Israelis want to hold on to the "Fruits of Victory" in 1967? What is Abba Eiban implying and what might he consider a "satisfactory peace"? **(5)**

4 "The Six Day War arose from the exaggerated mutual fears of attack felt by Israel and by her immediate Arab neighbours." Using the sources and from your own knowledge, do you agree with this verdict? Explain your answer. **(10)**

Total marks = 27

Answers

Clearly, simple knowledge of the **facts** is not enough. Skills needed here include the ability to **read carefully** and **comprehend** passages drawn from contemporary documents. Also the ability to **scrutinise** and **interpret** visual evidence and to **sift** and **compare** evidence for **reliability, bias, accuracy** etc. is needed.

Be aware of the advantages and disadvantages of **eye witness** and **contemporary evidence**. It may be close to the action and may be vivid, but often it is too close, particularly in wartime. Yet, accounts written a long time after the event may be poorly remembered, or distorted by hindsight.

Watch out for the **type of passage**. Is it a speech? If so, to whom? Who is it trying to impress? Is it a private letter? Or a business one? Or a diary? Does the author expect the document to become public?

Example one:

The first source is clearly a propaganda poster which certainly indicates official Nazi attitudes to women – though, being propaganda, it may well be a distorted or exaggerated viewpoint of Goebbels' or Hitler's personal opinions. There is no indication of to whom Goebbels is writing in the second example. The third source is a publicly remembered part of a conversation and probably a snippet of genuinely and informally expressed opinions.

The questions require **intelligent reading and viewing** of the sources. Comment upon the image portrayed by the motherly figure and infant in Source A and compare it with Goebbels' little biology lesson. There are clear implications for both sexes. Goebbels visualises the male role in simple biological terms – aggression towards the enemy, defence of the female. Hitler's comment is equally simple and rings chillingly true. A good answer will perhaps suggest to the examiner that the fate of the small child is also mapped out, whatever its gender. Using your own knowledge, point out what the actual treatment of male and female Germans was during the war, and indicate how the different sexes were educated in schools and in the Hitler Youth and the League of German Girls.

Example two:

This is very much about bias. Your answers need you to see each piece of evidence from the different viewpoints of Arab and Israeli. Is the photograph propaganda or documentary? Could it be propaganda for either side? Israelis could use it to frighten their compatriots with tales of gun-toting fanatical children! Arabs would use it to emphasise the story of defensive Arabs working even as children to defend themselves against Israeli aggression.

Likewise, you should know who Nasser was and why he was important, and the examiner may ask you directly about him, but even if you did not know you should be able to spot the bias behind Nasser's account of the origins of the war. Similarly you should be able to deduce that the Israeli Foreign Minister will imply that the Arabs have been aggressive, that Israel by "giving up the fruits of victory" has been made vulnerable. Finally, be aware of the equation underlying time spent on these questions and the number of marks available. Six marks at stake in reading and commenting on a source may reveal six or three points to be made. Be alert, don't spend too long chasing too few marks, and remember that when the question asks you to look at sources as well as using your own knowledge – **Do Both**.